Basic
ACCOUNTING

J Randall Stott

revised by Mike Truman

TEACH YOURSELF BOOKS

Coventry University

A catalogue record for this title is available from the British Library

ISBN 0 340 69776 8

First published 1985
Second Edition 1997

Impression number   10 9   8   7   6   5   4   3   2   1
Year   2001   2000   1999   1998   1997

Typeset by Transet Limited, Coventry, England.

Printed in Great Britain for Hodder & Stoughton Educational, a division of Hodder Headline Plc, 338 Euston Road, London NW1 3BH by Cox & Wyman Limited, Reading, Berkshire.

PO 98010215
14-12-98

CONTENTS

1

INTRODUCTION

There is nothing magical about book-keeping and accounting. The *keeping of accounts* simply involves the routine recording of business transactions, the exchange and the payment for both goods and services being identified by money values.

The accounting device and method explained in this textbook is called 'double entry book-keeping'. Sometimes referred to as the *arithmetic of commerce*, it is a form of simple arithmetic – that is all.

The purpose of accounting

We live in a world of credit. Without some form of accounting record, indecision and confusion would result. Not only is it businesslike to keep accounts as a check on suppliers and credit customers, but the financial statements made up from these accounting records keep management informed, from time to time, of the progress of their businesses.

The financial statements are scrutinised and verified when:

- a business is sold or a new partner is admitted to an existing firm
- a bank loan or a substantial overdraft is needed by the business
- the local Inspector of Taxes assesses the income tax liability on the trading results of the business

Business transactions involving all aspects of production, trade and distribution are varied and voluminous in every town and village. The bulk of these transactions are on credit, the settlement for the merchandise bought or for the services used often being delayed for a few days or a few weeks. It is important that there is printed or written evidence of the original terms and money values agreed upon between producer and consumer, vendor and credit customer, or the professional service-provider and the client.

In double entry book-keeping, the money values of all transactions with suppliers of goods on credit (the **creditors**) and the sales to credit customers (the **debtors**) are recorded. The details of all money received and money paid, whether by cheque or in cash, are also recorded in a manner which, with practice, becomes routine and easy to comprehend.

Some everyday terms take on a different meaning when used in the accounting sense. A few of these terms are now introduced.

- **Assets** refer to the property and possessions of a business, which may be owned by an individual (a sole trader or one-person business), a firm or partnership, or perhaps a limited company. In this elementary textbook, book-keeping is explained as it would be adapted to the financial accounting side of a sole trader's business. Nevertheless, basic principles of double entry, throughout the world of commerce, remain the same.
  - *Fixed assets* are those assets which are retained for the benefit and permanent use of the business, such as premises, machinery and plant, vehicles, fixtures and fittings. These assets are not for re-sale in the trading sense.
  - *Current or circulating assets* change their form in the course of trading, common examples being stock of goods for sale, the trae debts of customers, money in the bank and office cash.

- **Liabilities** are the debts and obligations of the business, the external and trade liabilities falling into two main categories:
  - *fixed liabilities* such as a mortgage or a long-term loan,
  - *current liabilities* comprising outstanding accounts owing to trade and expense creditors, and sometimes a bank overdraft.

In addition to the external debts and obligations of the business, there is generally a large internal debt owing by the business to its proprietor under the heading of **capital**. This, in the case of a sole trader, would be regarded, on the basis of the account book figures, as the equity of the proprietors or the net worth of the business.

— Balance sheet: an introduction —

The main consideration, normally, to be given to any new business venture, even one based at home, is that of finance, money or financial backing. A trading business needs substantial funds or extended credit facilities from the outset. A place has to be found for the storage and safety of merchandise, and thought needs to be given to deliveries (involving transport), communications (post, telephone and perhaps e-mail), and the recording of cash and credit dealings (the book work and accounts). In addition, at least some small reserve of finance is required to maintain oneself during the initial period of creating or developing the business.

Before we start on the routine book work of a typical small trader, we shall take a glimpse at one of the targets and main end-products of this short course in elementary accounting. This is a financial statement called the **balance sheet**.

Suppose your great-aunt Sarah recently bequeathed you a legacy of £500. You decide to be 'your own boss' and work up some kind of small trading connection from your home address.

With effect from 1 June, this £500 is allocated to your new business venture to become the sole asset and property of the business in your name. The business, regarded as a unit and entity separate from you personally, acknowledges its debt and obligation to you, as owner and proprietor, in this commencing balance sheet, thus:

Balance Sheet as at 1 June

Assets employed			You may have other sources of income and property of your own, but that is your private affair, quite distinct from this new trading venture now being financed by your investment of £500.
	£		
Cash in hand	500		
Financed by			
	£		
Proprietary capital	500		

The proprietor's holding or control over the net assets of a business is sometimes referred to as the **owner's equity**.

The routine business dealings of a small retail trader are called transactions. Generally, they involve the purchase and sale of merchandise for cash and/or credit (where payment is delayed), the settlement of trade and expense accounts for goods bought and for services used, and occasionally the purchase of a 'fixed asset' for the retention and permanent use of the business.

During the first week of June a number of transactions take place, and in this particular instance a separate balance sheet has been drawn up simply to illustrate how this financial statement is *affected in two ways by each transaction*. Normally, though, the listing and grouping of assets and liabilities on a balance sheet would be made in greater detail at the end of the trading period, perhaps every six months or only once a year.

2 June You pay £130 for two large storage cupboards and some strong shelving.

NB The four stages of these elementary balance sheets are explained by simple arithmetic. The routine debit/credit procedure starts in Chapter 4.

Balance Sheet as at 2 June

Assets employed	£	Property has been acquired for permanent use by the business. This purchase is shown as a 'fixed asset'. Cash is decreased by the sum paid out.
Fixed assets		
Fittings/fixtures	130	
Current assets		
Cash in hand	370	The payment for the fixed asset does not affect the holding of the proprietor (his capital) nor current liabilities, as the business at this stage has no outside debts.
	500	
Financed by	£	
Proprietary capital	500	
Current liabilities		
	500	

3 June You buy merchandise on credit priced at £200 from Wholesalers Ltd, arranging to pay for the goods bought later in the month.

Balance Sheet as at 3 June

Assets employed			
Fixed assets		£	
Fittings/fixtures		130	
Current assets	£		
Stock	200		
Cash in hand	370	570	
		700	
Financed by			
		£	
Proprietary capital		500	
Current liabilities			
Trade creditors		200	
		700	

Goods to the value of £200 have been taken into stock at *cost price*, increasing current assets to £570. These goods have been bought on credit (no money has been paid). So cash remains at £370.

There is still no change in the owner's capital account. However, an outside liability has been incurred of £200. The individual names of trade creditors do not appear on the balance sheet.

4 June You sell goods priced at £60 to a cash customer, and further goods priced at £40 to a credit customer (to be paid at the end of the month).

Say profit mark-up is 25% on cost, i.e. 20% on the selling price. The cost of the goods sold is thus £80.

Balance Sheet as at 4 June

Assets employed			
Fixed assets		£	
Fittings/fixtures		130	
Current assets	£		
Stock	120		
Trade debtors	40		
Cash	430	590	
		720	
Financed by			
		£	
Capital 1 June	500		
Add profit	20	520	
Current liabilities			
Trade creditors		200	
		720	

£80 of stock (at cost) is sold for £100. This leaves stock balance in hand at £120.

The cash position is now £370 + £60 = £430.

Amount due from credit customer (£40) is shown under 'trade debtors'.

The difference between the cost price £80 and the selling price of £100 is the **trading profit**. This is added to the proprietor's capital as the reward for investment.

5 June You pay £50 off your supplier's account for the goods bought on 3 June, and then withdraw £25 cash for your own private and personal use.

Balance Sheet as at 5 June

Assets employed			
Fixed assets		£	
Fittings/fixtures		130	
Current assets	£		
Stock	120		
Trade debtors	40		
Cash	355	515	
		645	
Financed by			
	£		
Capital 1 June	500		
Add profit	20		
	520		
Less drawings	25	495	
Current liabilities			
Trade creditors		150	
		645	

The £50 paid off trade creditor's account reduces *both* the business cash and the amount of the trade liabilities total. The stock figure is not affected by this payment.

The sum of £25 withdrawn for the proprietor's own use is called 'drawings'. Business cash is reduced and also the proprietor's holding or net assets as shown by his capital account.

Note how the proprietor's capital account of this small business remains constant until affected by:

- business profits or losses
- withdrawals by the proprietor (and it would of course be increased by additional private capital paid into the business).

Some elementary accounting concepts have been touched upon in this short balance-sheet preamble. At each stage there is the emphasis upon total assets equalling total liabilities (including the capital). The accounting equation $A = C + L$ applies all the way through, where:

A represents the total assets of the business
C the proprietary capital and
L the external debts and liabilities of the business.

Practical work

Like learning to use a computer keyboard, book-keeping is a 'doing' subject. The progress of the student is geared to his or her capacity and inclination for work. At the beginning, a fair amount or repetition is necessary to encourage the development of correct habits. Attention to detail is continually stressed, and once the basic principles have been established, new procedures are built in stage by stage.

In the classroom, the teacher will probably supplement the textbook explanation by simple blackboard or OHP illustrations, and students will then work through similar exercises from the textbook.

At this stage the text should be re-read, and then the remaining exercises of the chapter completed and checked against the brief answers at the back of the book.

2

THE LEDGER SYSTEM

The ledger system of double entry book-keeping entails the use of a number of account-ruled books (known as a set of books) for the purpose of recording accurate information, in money values, of the day-to-day trading operations of a business. From these permanent records, periodical statements are prepared to show the trading profit or loss made by the business and its estimated net worth, at any given date.

In the past, these records would quite literally have been kept in bound ledger books. However, even before the widespread introduction of computers, mechanised systems based upon mechanical accounting machines were used by many larger companies. In smaller organisations, looseleaf systems with multipart forms and carbon paper reduced the number of times that book-keepers had to write out the same data.

Now any business with a full-time book-keeper is likely to have computerised its accounting. However, computerisation can only speed up the arithmetic of accounting, it cannot replace an understanding of the concepts. Underlying all modern computer accounting programs is the same double entry system described in this book.

Ledger accounts

The record of trading transactions is kept, in money value, on the folios or pages of these account books, called **ledgers**. The ledger folios have special rulings to suit the needs of the business. The bank statement style (page 59) lends itself to modern accounting, but for the time being double entry will be explained by the older traditional method. This is the ordinary ruling for the older style of ledger account:

Name of Account

Debit or left-hand side				Credit or right-hand side			
Date	Value COMING IN		£	Date	Value GOING OUT		£

In practice, separate ledgers are kept for the different classes of accounts (customers, suppliers, business property, trading revenue and expense, etc.). Batches or groups of similar accounts are kept together, and ledgers are indexed so that information with regard to any particular account may quickly be obtained.

The cash account

The cash account is first explained as *part of the ledger system*. Some students may already be familiar with the simple recording of receipts and payments of money.

Assume that you start in business (a small retail shop) on 1 June with *£200 cash as your commencing capital*. At present we shall only deal in currency notes and coin: cheque and bank transactions will be explained later.

During the month of June all your business dealings are for cash. The details of your trading transactions are listed below, and then posted or entered in your **cash account** for the month of June as the first stage of a book-keeping exercise involving the *receipt and payment of money only*. Note that at this stage there are no credit transactions.

June		£
2	Goods bought for re-sale	75.00
5	Money received for goods sold	45.80
12	Paid for classified advertising	7.30
18	Cash takings (i.e. cash sales)	56.20
20	Bought further goods for cash	85.00
24	Cash sales	110.50
30	Paid salary to temporary assistant	60.00
	Withdrew cash for private use (this is called **drawings**)	50.00

The cash account is now made up for the month of June, all money *received* being **debited**, and all money *paid* being **credited**. Note the one-word description of all the credit entries, and the complete absence of the words 'cash' and 'paid' on this side, because all these entries refer to **cash payments**.

Dr. (debit)   **Cash Account**   (credit) Cr.

Date	Money COMING IN	£		Date	Money PAID OUT	£	
June				June			
1	Balance in hand	200	00	2	Purchases	75	00
5	Cash sales	45	80	12	Advertising	7	30
18	Cash sales	56	20	20	Purchases	85	00
24	Cash sales	110	50	30	Salary	60	00
				30	Drawings	50	00

Explanatory notes

1 The cash in hand, a debit balance at 1 June, is your commencing capital in this particular instance, being the sole asset and property possessed by the business on this date. In later exercises it will be seen that business property *in money* is normally *only part of the proprietor's capital*.

2 Cash takings or cash sales refer to the normal and continuous 'across the counter' sales of the small retailer, in contrast to any **credit sales** where the possession of the goods passes from vendor to buyer at the time of the sale, with the settlement and payment being deferred until later. In these early exercises we are concerned only with cash purchases and cash sales.

3 The narrow column on the left of each cash column is used for cross-referencing to the appropriate and corresponding account of the double entry (explained in Chapter 4).

4 Goods and merchandise bought by the business to be re-sold are called **purchases**, distinguishing this heavy prime cost from the other many and varied expenses of trading, and also to show a clear distinction between this basic trading expense and the acquisition cost of property and assets such as machinery and fixtures, bought for the retention and permanent use of the business.

5 The one-word description, as far as possible, of each entry, is important, as this serves to identify the opposite and corresponding double entry, normally in another ledger.

6 The posting of all amounts *coming into* an account on the **debit side**, and all amounts *paid or going out* of an account on the **credit**

side, avoids the necessity for continual addition and subtraction until the balancing-up stage, generally at the end of the month.

Assignments

> ## KEY POINTS
>
> 1 Centre the heading of the cash account and leave a blank space between the heading and the details within the account.
> 2 The name of the month need not be repeated once it is placed at the top of the date column, but the date of each transaction must be given.
> 3 The £ sign need only be shown at the top of each cash column, and should not appear against the individual receipts and payments.
> 4 As far as possible, use a single one-word explanation of the entry in the details part of the account.
> 5 The words 'received' and 'paid' are superfluous in the details section, and the word 'cash' need only appear on the debit in order to distinguish cash sales from any sales on credit (which are not posted to the cash account).
> 6 The correct and *vertical* alignment of the figures in the money columns will make additions easier at the balancing-up stage.
> 7 The main rule for all cash accounts is:
>   (a) debit money *coming in*
>   (b) credit money *paid out.*

2.1 You are required to post up the transactions listed below in a cash account for the first week of March.

March		£
1	Balance of cash in hand	40.00
3	Cash takings	26.44
4	Paid for further goods	14.80
	Paid advertising account	10.50
5	Cash sales	46.02
	Bought further supplies	16.60
6	Wages paid for temporary assistance	25.00

2.2 Give three good reasons for the permanent recording of business transactions.

3

BALANCING THE CASH BOOK

In book-keeping the term 'balancing' simply means adding up both the debit and the credit sides of an account, and deducting the smaller side (of less total value) from the larger side. The difference between the two sides is called the **balance** of the account.

Later it will be seen that the cash account is kept in a special ledger called the cash book, which, in practice, would probably be balanced weekly, and certainly at the end of every month.

The cash account on page 10 is reproduced here and balanced up in the ordinary way. Study the illustration and then read carefully the following instructions on balancing. The payments shown are after any discount allowed – this is explained in Chapter 13.

Dr. (debit)   **Cash Account (1)**   (credit) Cr.

Date	Money COMING IN		£		Date	Money PAID OUT		£	
June					June				
1	Balance in hand	2	200	00	2	Purchases	5	75	00
5	Cash sales	15	45	80	12	Advertising	8	7	30
18	Cash sales	15	56	20	20	Purchases	5	85	00
24	Cash sales	15	110	50	30	Salary	9	60	00
					30	Drawings	4	50	00
					30	Balance c/d		135	00
			412	50				412	50
July									
1	Balance b/d		135	20					

Note that there are fewer items on the debit of this cash account, and spaces have been left blank to allow for neatness and to ensure that the *corresponding totals are on the same horizontal level*.

The **folio** or page numbers relating to the opposite and corresponding double entry have been inserted in the narrow folio column in front of each amount, prior to the posting of the double entry in the separate ledger accounts as shown in the next chapter. For clarity, the folio or page number is shown in brackets after the name of each ledger account in these early stages.

The balance of cash in hand at 30 June (£135.20) is the difference between the debit total of £412.50 and the total of the payments (£277.30). This balancing figure of £135.20 is inserted as an additional item on the *credit side above the total*. The two totals now agree and are ruled off in the manner shown. The total of the payments (£277.30) before balancing may be noted in pencil, but *is not inked-in* as a permanent feature.

The difference or balance on an account should never be left suspended in mid-air. In the case of the cash account, the balance will be entered as the last item on the credit side above the total, and then *brought down below the debit total on the opposite side*. The two totals are ruled off neatly on the same horizontal level, the lower line of the total being double ruled.

The abbreviations **c/d** and **b/d** signify 'carried down' and 'brought down', and where balances or totals are sometimes carried forward from one folio to another, the abbreviations **c/f** and **b/f** denote 'carried forward' and 'brought forward'.

The physical cash balance must always be a *debit balance* as money can only be paid out of an available fund or balance in hand.

Assignments

KEY POINTS

1 First make your additions in pencil and ink-in afterwards. In balancing, remember to deduct the total of the payments from the total of the receipts, only inserting the *difference* (which is the balance) on the *credit side above the total* on the right-hand side of the cash account.
2 Bring down the same amount shown on the credit side above as a *debit balance now below the total on the left-hand side* of the account. This debit balance is simply the excess receipts over payments.

---

3 Cash account totals must be on the same horizontal level, and the lower line should be double-ruled to indicate a total.

4 With a little concentration, these simple cash book exercises will quickly teach you how to record elementary cash transactions, leading on to the routine of ledger posting.

5 In assignment 3.3, although payments are mentioned to a supplier and by two credit customers, we are only concerned at this stage with how the money received and the money paid affects your cash position. The earlier part of this kind of transaction (the credit purchase and the credit sales) is explained later in the text.

3.1 What is the purpose of the two columns on the left and the right of the ledger, debit always being on the left and credit always being on the right?

What kind of receipts and payments would be found in the cash book of:

| a confectioner | a plumber |
| a dentist | an accountant? |

3.2 Post up the transactions shown in a cash account for the month of September, rule off the account, and bring down the new balance as at 1 October.

Sept.		£
1	Cash balance	200.00
2	Bought goods for cash	35.60
4	Receipts from customers	42.10
8	Paid rent for month	30.00
10	Cash takings	10.50
	Paid advertising account	16.40
12	Cash sales to date	38.28
	Stationery supplies bought	12.60
18	Cash takings	28.48
20	Further purchases for re-sale	19.36
22	Paid carriage on purchases	2.25
	Paid part-time assistant	56.00
28	Withdrew for private expenses	30.00

3.3 At the close of business on 30 June you have £300 in cash, your only asset and commencing cash balance for the month of July.

Your daily cash sales for July total £168.50. Two old customers pay their outstanding accounts (Marcia Moore £23.40 and Lesley Lane £35.60) on 5 July. You pay your own supplier Robert Reese & Son £52.50 on 20 July for deliveries during June. Other payments made in July were:

July		£
3	Rent	40.00
11	Petrol/oil	12.50
15	Stationery	8.36
28	Salaries	48.00

On 25 July you withdrew £50 from the business to go on a theatre trip. From this information, you are asked to post up a cash account for the month of July bringing down your cash balance on 1 August.

4

DOUBLE ENTRY THEORY AND PRACTICE

The cash account shown in Chapter 3 is two-sided like all ledger accounts, but this is not the meaning of double entry book-keeping. Each entry in the cash account, whether receipt or payment, has only one aspect.

The cash account itself is a useful device for recording money received and money paid, and periodical balancing up will reveal and check the physical cash in hand, but the cash book figures alone cannot be used as a true guide to finding out the trading profit or loss of a business.

With the ascertainment of business profit in view, we now identify and record the opposite or dual aspect of each cash account entry as it is posted to another ledger account.

— First principles of double entry —

In all business transactions there are *two separate and distinct aspects* to be recorded within the same accounting period. Two separate accounts are involved in each transaction, one account recording the debit (receiving) aspect, the other recording the credit (giving or paying) aspect.

> The account *receiving value or benefit is debited.*
> The account *giving, paying or relinquishing benefit is credited.*

Sometimes it is easier to decide or identify the account (or person) giving up something of value. This will determine the *credit part* of the two aspects and at the same time serve to identify the *related debit*.

Dr.	Name of first account					Cr.
Date	**Debit what comes into the account** (value received)	£		Date	**Credit what goes out** (value paid or relinquished)	£

Dr.	Name of second account					Cr.
Date	**Debit what comes into the account** (value received)	£		Date	**Credit what goes out** (value paid or relinquished)	£

Practical book-keeping

In the previous chapter, only one aspect of double entry was recorded with regard to each item in the cash account. The opposite and dual aspect of each entry is shown on the related ledger accounts.

The reason for the one-word description of most of the postings in the cash account will now be understood, as these are the *names and headings of the new ledger accounts*.

In practice, the postings from the cash account to the related ledger accounts would be made in date order, but for ease in explanation, all debit items will be dealt with first, and then the credit items.

——— Capital and net worth ———

The first entry in your cash account is the commencing cash in hand, a balance of £200 at 1 June. You have given or loaned this business £200, which from this date becomes the sole asset and property of the business. This is also your own *personal contribution* to the business, and in consequence will be credited to your **capital account** to show that you now have a financial stake or holding in this business of the net worth of £200 at 1 June.

Thus the posting of this first item of £200 to the credit of capital account initiates the double entry to the opposite side of another ledger account.

Dr.					Capital Account (2)				Cr.
				June 1	Cash	CB1	£ 200	00	

—— Cash sales or daily takings ——

The remaining three entries on the debit side of the cash account are all for cash sales or daily cash takings. These individual daily sales are posted to the **credit of sales account** for the month of June, and in due course this grouped information will be used to work out the trading profit for the month. In practice, the postings would be made day by day.

Dr.   **Sales Account (15)**   Cr.

				June			£	
				5	Cash	CB1	45	80
				18	Cash	CB1	56	20
				24	Cash	CB1	110	50

Now we turn to the *credit* side of the cash account where the nature of the entries is a little more varied. All items on this side refer to payments for merchandise bought, trading expenses incurred, whilst 'drawings' indicates that some money has been withdrawn by the proprietor for personal or private use.

—— Goods bought for re-sale ——

Goods may be bought for stock or conversion into products for sale to the general public. In any event, a clear distinction must be made between goods bought as the stock in trade of a business and the property (assets) and everyday trading expenses of the business. Goods bought for re-sale are termed 'purchases' and thus the payments made on 2 June and 20 June are posted to the *debit* side of the purchases account.

Dr.   **Purchases Account (5)**   Cr.

June			£					
2	Cash	CB1	75	00				
20	Cash	CB1	85	00				

—— Trading expenses ——

The various trading expenses for the month of June (in this instance only advertising and salaries) are debited to *separate accounts*, thus completing their double entry.

Dr. **Advertising Account (8)** Cr.

June 12	Cash	CB1	£ 7	30				

Dr. **Salaries Account (9)** Cr.

June 30	Cash	CB1	£ 60	00				

— Money withdrawn for private use —

The remaining credit item of £50 for drawings is not a business expense. It is a withdrawal by the proprietor of part of the money invested in the business, although in the case of profitable businesses the owner would regard such withdrawals to be in anticipation of excess revenue or profit. Nevertheless, since part of the business assets (cash) is reduced, there is also a reduction of the proprietor's holding (capital account). Sums withdrawn will temporarily be debited to the drawings account, and at the end of the trading period be *transferred* to the debit of the capital account.

Dr. **Drawings Account (4)** Cr.

June 30	Cash	CB1	£ 50	00				

In this small exercise and introduction to double entry the word 'cash' has been used throughout in the body of each account, simply indicating that the original posting or entry has come from the cash account (or **cash book** as it will shortly be called). At this elementary stage, the cash book is our main and only **book of original entry**, but as we proceed through the various phases of accounting procedures, it will be seen that the initiation stage is not always from the cash book.

In the practical world of commerce, financial transactions are varied and voluminous, and generally involve much larger sums than are used either here or throughout the rest of this book. Nevertheless, the basic principles of double entry accounting remain the same.

Pause for thought

- Consider now the use and purpose of the folio columns, those narrow columns in front of the main cash columns. What is the accounting term used for entering or making the dual entry from one account to another?

● How would you decide which account should be debited and which account should be credited?

● Is it possible to finish with the cash balance *brought down underneath* the total on the credit side of the cash columns?

Assignments

KEY POINTS

1 Financial information is being grouped at this stage, in total form, for the use of the accountant and management. By this means, the task of the accounts department is made easier in the preparation of various financial statements.

2 Do not cramp the writing-up of your ledger accounts in an effort to economise on paper. Leave a space of several lines between accounts.
   Again, remember to leave a space between each ledger account heading and the details in the account.

3 Do not scratch out or try to rub out any wrong figures. Use 'white out' liquid very sparingly, and be careful to let it dry before writing over it. In practice, though, it is often best simply to rule through incorrect amounts, inserting the correct figure above the error.

4 As far as possible, reduce the description of the money value received or paid to one word, as this will be the heading of the opposite or contra account as a rule.

5 Use the £ sign only at the top of the cash columns, and do not repeat the name of the month once inserted at the top of the debit or credit columns within the same account.

6 Number the various ledger accounts in assignment 4.2 and give some thought to the cross-referencing procedure between

---

4.1 Study the cash account of Mark Clark now shown, and then answer the questions underneath.

(*a*) What is meant by 'Balance b/f?

(*b*) Explain each item in date order.

(*c*) Distinguish between cash sales and the sales to credit customers.

(*d*) Why is information about purchases shown separately from other expenses?

(e) Again, why are the payments for salaries and 'drawings for self' not combined?

(f) Balance up this cash account, and post up the double entry to the corresponding ledger accounts.

Dr.				**Cash Account**			Cr.
June		£		June		£	
1	Balance b/f	175	00	2	Purchases	120	00
9	Cash sales	39	80	5	Adverts.	15	60
14	Cash sales	66	45	9	Garage a/c	12	85
22	Cash sales	52	35	18	Self	30	00
28	Cash sales	84	40	25	Salaries	112	25
				30	Rent for June	35	00

4.2 Make up the cash account of Janina Jones from her cash transactions, shown below, for the month of January.

Jan.		£
1	Cash in hand	250.00
2	Bought goods to be sold	66.60
	Paid for stamps	8.20
5	Cash takings	54.48
12	Paid salaries	64.00
	Withdrew for 'self'	30.00
14	Sundry expenses	14.15
18	Cash takings	84.94
	Paid insurance	12.50
22	Drawings	30.00
28	Paid salaries	64.00
30	Telephoned Thomas Hudson for urgent delivery of stock	
	Consignment received the next day, invoiced at £44.50	

After balancing up Miss Jones' cash account for January, post the double entry to the related account in her ledger.

5

THE TRIAL BALANCE

The next stage, after the completion of the postings, is the extraction from the books of all balances on a statement called the **trial balance**. It is *not* an account.

The financial information, classified and grouped in the various ledger accounts in the last chapter, is now totalled on each account, and the debit and credit *balances* listed on the trail balance, including the *final balance of the cash account*.

Trial Balance   30 June

		Debit £	Credit £
Cash balance	CB1	135.20	
Capital	L2		200.00
Sales	15		212.50
Purchases	5	160.00	
Advertising	8	7.30	
Salaries	9	60.00	
Drawings	4	50.00	
		412.50	412.50

There is no particular order for the grouping of the account balances, but to avoid omission it is suggested that the final cash balance should be extracted first, and the remainder of the ledger balances may then be listed in either page or book sequence.

There is no complication about double entry here, at this has been completed. Debit balances are merely listed on the debit of the trial balance, and credit balances on the credit.

—— **Purpose of the trial balance** ——

It is emphasised that the trial balance is not an account. It is not part of the double entry, but merely a list of debit and credit balances taken from the books, normally at the end of a specific trading period (which may be a month, six months or often one year) for the purpose of:

- checking the arithmetical accuracy of the postings, and
- rendering the work of the accountant or book-keeper easier in the making up of financial summaries, often with a view to the preparation of revenue trading accounts, together with a balance sheet.

Note that only the balances of the accounts are bought on to the trial balance. For example, the debit balance of £135.20 is extracted from the cash account, and *not the two totals* for receipts and payments.

The sales account is totalled to show total sales of £212.50 for the month, which in effect is the credit balance taken to the trial balance. Similarly with the purchases, and so on.

If no mistakes have been made in posting the cash book to the various ledger accounts (debit for credit and vice versa), the sum total of the debit balances on the trial balance should equal the sum total of the credit balances.

Trial balance totals do not agree

If the trial balance totals do not agree, you should try to find the error. It is often useful to calculate the difference between the totals. You may find that this gives a figure that you can find in the original list of balances and which you have either not included in the trial balance, or have not included in your addition of the trial balance figures.

If this is not the case, try halving the difference (if it is 'even') and seeing if a balance of that amount has been included in the wrong side of trial balance, where it will have a double impact in the discrepancy.

Finally, try dividing the difference by nine. If it divides exactly, you may have made a transposition error, for example entering 1985 rather than 1895.

Assignments

KEY POINTS

1   With practice you will acquire an automatic thinking habit of 'debit this account' and 'credit that account' and comprehension will become as easy as simple arithmetic.

2   The trial balance is *not* an account. It is simply a list of debit and credit balances assembled by the book-keeper to prove the arithmetical accuracy of his postings.

3   Every *account balance* in the books is brought on to the trial balance, including the *closing balance of cash in hand*.

4   When the trial balance does not balance:

(a)   Check the trial balance additions again. Your figures may be out of alignment.

(b)   Check all additions again, in particular those in the cash book, and those of the purchases and sales accounts.

(c)   Make sure that the *closing cash balance* has been brought to the *debit* of the trial balance.

(d)   Check the double entry of all postings in the books, *debit for credit*, and re-check the extraction of the balances to their correct side of the trial balance.

5.1   Assemble the information shown below in trial balance form, and ascertain the capital or net worth of this business at 31 December by deducting the total credit balances from the total debit balances.

	£
Cash in hand 31 Dec.	225
Advertising expenses	65
Purchases for December	4500
Sales for December	5750
Rent and rates paid	360
Stationery bought	40
Salaries paid	880
Drawings for month	400

5.2   Enter up the transactions shown below in your cash book and post the double entry to the ledger accounts. Balance the accounts where necessary, and prove the arithmetical accuracy of your postings by taking out a trial balance at 31 January.

Jan.		£
1	Cash in hand	300.00
2	Paid insurance	15.50
	Bought goods	120.00
6	Paid rent	30.00
8	Cash sales	38.80
11	Classified advertising	10.50
15	Paid salaries	60.00
	Bought stamps	5.00
18	Cash sales	56.20
22	Purchases	84.00
24	Petrol/oil	18.30
	Cash sales	42.10
28	Salaries	60.00
31	Drawings	50.00
	Cash sales	64.40

5.3 Explain the difference between salaries and drawings. Why is the Inland Revenue very much concerned about this distinction when checking the sole trader's year-end accounts?

REVISION EXERCISE 1

In this exercise you start with £400 cash as the sole asset or property of the business financed by you. The following transactions take place during the month of September.

Sept.		£
1	Arranged to pay a rent of £25 for the use of a small lock-up shop, and paid the landlord a month's rent in advance	25.00
3	Bought miscellaneous goods for sale	75.00
	Purchased stamps from Post Office	5.00
	Cash sales	55.74
6	Hired a part-time assistant and paid wages	30.00
	Paid for advertising in local paper	12.20
8	Cash sales	64.82
	Bought further goods for sale	45.40
	Paid carriage on purchases	4.50
10	Cash purchases	15.66
	Withdrew cash for household expenses	50.00
14	Paid wages	30.00
	Cash sales	54.30
18	Paid insurance premium for fire risk	16.60
	Cash sales	68.78
20	Paid wages	30.00
	Bought invoice stationery etc.	9.98
25	Cash takings for past three days	82.20
	Further purchases for stock	26.50
28	Paid wages	30.00
30	Cash withdrawn to pay private bills	50.00

Enter up these cash receipts and payments in your cash book for September, post up the corresponding double entry to the ledger accounts and take out a trial balance as at 30 September.

At what stage and date of the month was your cash balance, in its circulatory flow, at its highest and lowest ebb?

6

GROSS PROFIT AND STOCK

This small arithmetical problem explains how basic costs (including the adjustment for stocks) influence the selling price of commodities.

Say you have 10 articles which have cost you £1 each. You buy 20 more, also at £1, and sell 25 articles at £1.40 each. What profit have you made? Quickly, by mental arithmetic, you might say £5 profit (the excess of your sales receipts £35 over the total cost of the available stock you had for sale).

But what about the stock of articles not yet sold? This stock presumably has a very definite value and must be taken into account in working out your profit. It is valued at its cost price of £5 (i.e. five articles not yet sold which you bought at £1 each).

Arithmetically, the true profit is worked out thus:

		£
Total sales (25 articles at £1.40 each)		35.00
Add stock unsold (5 valued at £1 cost)		5.00
		40.00
Less stock at start (10 articles at £1)	£10.00	
and additional purchases (20 at £1)	20.00	30.00
Showing a final profit of		10.00

Another illustration is now shown, both arithmetically and in a proper accounting manner, leading on to the business trading account and gross profit.

A small trader, on 1 April, has a stock of 200 articles bought at the average cost of £1 each. Early in April he buys 100 more of these articles, now priced at £1.10 each. During the month of April he sells 240 articles at £1.50 each.

The trader's true profit is first worked out arithmetically in this way:

		£
Total sales (240 at £1.50)		360.00
Add stock unsold (60 at cost of £1.10)		66.00
		426.00
Less stock at start (200 at £1)	£200.00	
plus purchases during April		
(100 at £1.10)	110.00	310.00
To show a trading profit of		116.00

In accounting, the money values of this arithmetical problem would be set out in this way:

Trading Account for the month ended 30 April

	£		£
Opening stock 1 April	200.00	Net sales	360.00
Purchases for month	110.00	Closing stock 30 April	66.00
Gross profit	116.00		
	426.00		426.00

The older style of trading account shown above has now been superseded by a more modern style, disclosing the *cost of sales figure*, thus:

Trading Account for the month ended 30 April

	£		£
Stock 1 April	200.00	Net sales	360.00
Add purchases	110.00		
	310.00		
Less stock 30 April	66.00		
Cost of sales	244.00		
Gross profit	116.00		
	360.00		360.00

Note that the gross profit is unchanged by the variation in style. The older-style account is included here simply because it is easier to follow the double entries.

Cost of sales

The cost of the goods sold (commonly called the **cost of sales**) is found by adding purchases to the opening stock, and then deducting the closing stock at its valuation.

The purpose of the trading account is to find the main or gross profit (or loss) on trading for a certain stated period. The gross profit is simply the balance of the account, the difference between the net sales and the cost of sales.

Valuation of stock

In the commercial world, the valuation of the stock not yet sold at the close of an accounting period is taken to be either at its cost price (the price at which it was bought) *or* at the current market price, *whichever is the lower*. When working elementary exercises, students are given the closing stock figure as a rule, unless the problem is specifically based upon the calculation of stock. Even so, establishing the correct value is not always easy. If stocks cannot be identified to a particular purchase, and are simply kept in bulk, what cost price is used? Is it assumed that the first stocks bought were the first ones to be used, or that the last bought were the first used? In practice, the former (known as **FIFO** – first in, first out) is normally used, rather than the latter (known as **LIFO** – last in, first out).

The stock account

The commencing stock of an established business is already a debit balance in the books at the beginning of a new accounting period. It will have been debited to the stock account at its valuation at the close of the previous accounting period. Consequently the *old stock figure* of an established business is taken to the debit of the trial balance when final accounts are being prepared for the current trading period.

In examination papers, the new closing stock figure can always be identified by its date. Generally, the closing stock is brought into the books *after the trial balance stage*, by a new debit to the stock account and with its corresponding credit to the newly prepared trading account.

Note how the stock account below is made up from the information given earlier in this chapter. The opening stock (£200) at 1 April will be *transferred* from the debit of stock account to the debit of the trading account. This transfer is shown on the credit of the stock account, squaring off this part of the old account as at 30 April. At the same time, the £66 debit for the more recent valuation of closing stock at 30 April is now brought into the books for the first time by *creating a new debit* on this account and with its corresponding double entry being credited to the trading account, or, alternatively being deducted on the debit side of the trading account.

Dr.   **Stock Account**   Cr.

Apl.		£		Apl.		£	
1	Opening stock at beginning of month	200	00	30	Transfer of old stock to trading account	200	00
30	Trading account (closing stock now brought into the books)	66	00				

Assignments

KEY POINTS

1 The period covered by a trading account should always be given in its heading.

2 The dates of the two stocks (at the beginning and at the close of the trading period) should be shown, so that there is no confusion.

3 Assignment 6.1 simply involves a little arithmetic in finding the physical amount of closing stock. This will be valued at its last price, i.e. the price of the latest or most recent purchase. It is assumed that earlier stock bought is sold first.

4 Items of *prime cost* will be found on the debit of the trading account, the commencing stock figure, the net purchases, and the wages of production or of preparing the goods for sale. Also debited to the trading account will be expense items which vary with the turnover, such as carriage inwards or carriage on purchases.

5 On the credit of the trading account will be found the net sales and the closing stock, although the latter is more often shown as a deduction on the debit side to give the *cost of sales figure*.

6.1 Make up the trading account of Edwina Ewing, showing her cost of sales figure from the information given below.

May

At the beginning of the month there was a stock of certain articles on hand of 1800 items, bought at the average cost of £1 each. The total net purchases for May comprised 3400 articles bought at an average cost of £1.25.

Total net sales of 3800 articles realised £7300 from cash customers.

Ascertain Miss Ewing's final stock figure, place a valuation on it, and make up her trading account for May.

6.2 Extract the information you need from the trial balance below, to make up the trading account of Miss Vivette Green for the month of October.

Trial Balance of Vivette Green

31 October	£	£
Capital account 1 Oct.		2500
Drawings for month	180	
Net purchases	4800	
Net sales		6800
Carriage on purchases	50	
Warehousing expenses	220	
Stock 1 Oct.	1150	
Cash balance 31 Oct.	2900	
	9300	9300
Miss Green valued her closing stock on 31 October at £1550.		

6.3 What is the cost of sales figure in the preceding problem? Explain why, although recent purchases will comprise much of the closing stock valuation, the figure for net purchases is quite a different amount than the cost of goods sold.

7

TRADING AND PROFIT AND LOSS ACCOUNTS

In the preparation of the final accounts, the profit element is split, for convenience, into two parts:

- the **gross profit**, already described as the difference between the cost of sales and the actual sales total
- the **net profit**, which is the final trading profit of a business, after all office, general and distribution expenses have been charged against the gross profit brought down from trading account.

Illustration by arithmetic

Another arithmetical example is shown. Say a trader buys £500 of goods for sale. She pays £10 delivery costs and sells the whole consignment for £780, after incurring office and distribution expenses of £120. Arithmetically, her gross and net profit would be worked out in this way:

		£
Net sales on the whole consignment		780
Less purchases and	£500	
delivery costs	10	510
To give a gross profit of		270
Less office and distribution expenses		120
To show a final net profit of		150

In this illustration the commencing and closing stocks have been omitted for the sake of simplicity.

—— Making up the final accounts ——

Let us now refer back to the trial balance in Chapter 5 and make up a trading and profit and loss account from those details which relate specifically to the revenue income or expenditure of the business, namely purchases, sales, advertising and salaries.

Since this business was started from scratch, there is no opening stock, but it would be reasonable to assume that some stock would be unsold at the end of the first month's trading. If we place a valuation on the stock of purchases not yet sold of £80, the trading and profit and loss account will be made up on these lines.

Trading and Profit and Loss Account
for the month ended 30 June

	£		£
Stock 1 June	nil	Sales for month	212.50
Purchases for month	160.00	Stock 30 June	80.00
Gross profit c/d	132.50		
	292.50		292.50
Advertising	7.30	Gross profit b/d	132.50
Salaries	60.00		
Net profit	65.20		
	132.50		132.50

The trading and profit and loss account is really two separate accounts with a combined heading. These are the main revenue accounts of the business, the excess sales revenue (in the form of gross profit) being taken down to the credit of the lower account, an appendage or extension of the trading account. The gross trading profit is reduced, often substantially, in the profit and loss account, by a varied office, selling and administrative expenses of the business, the resultant figure being the net profit (and occasionally a net loss). Note that *net profit is a credit balance* of this lower account, whereas a *net loss would be a debit balance.*

Although the account set out in this way is easy to follow, it is invariably set out in vertical format in modern financial statements, looking like this:

	£	£
Sales per month		212.50
Less cost of sales:		
Purchases per month	160.00	
Plus opening stock	–	
Less closing stock	80.00	
		80.00
Gross profit		132.50
Advertising	7.30	
Salaries	60.00	
		67.30
Net profit		65.20

— Business revenue and expense —

The only figures extracted from the trial balance in Chapter 5 to make up the revenue account were those affecting the firm's trading profits. Three important balances were excluded in working out the business profit, namely *capital, drawings* and *cash*. A simple illustration will explain this:

Suppose you have £10 in your pocket. You buy £8 worth of goods, incur selling expenses of £3, and then dispose of your entire stock for £15. Your profit is £4 (£15 sales less £8 purchases plus £3 expenses).

Total sales		£15.00	
Less purchases	£8.00		
and expenses	3.00	11.00 = £4.00 profit	

Now if you consider this problem carefully, it will be seen that your original capital of £10 has not figured in your profit calculation, and neither has your final cash balance entered into it.

Also, if you had withdrawn £1 cash to buy your small sister some sweets, this sum would certainly have reduced your cash balance, but it would have *no effect upon the profit already made*.

Two kinds of carriage

Carriage on purchases (**carriage inwards**) is an additional expense on the goods bought, increasing the cost of the materials or commodities, and, as such, is a trading account expense.

Carriage on sales (**carriage outwards**) is a selling and distribution expense and is debited to the profit and loss section along with the many and varied administration and distribution expenses.

Note that both aspects of carriage are *debits*, and must not be confused with returns inwards and returns outwards explained in Chapter 15.

Production wages and office salaries

The wages of production or of warehousing (where merchandise is prepared for sale) vary with the turnover of the business, and are debited to the trading account as part of the cost of the goods produced.

The salaries of the office and administrative staff are charged to the profit and loss account. Like other routine expenses such as rent, rates and insurance, salaries are a more constant figure and not so much affected by short term variation of production volume.

On no account must the amounts spent upon the purchase of fixed assets and business property such as machinery, motor vehicles, fixtures and equipment be debited to either of these revenue accounts. Later, though, it will be explained that a kind of 'wear and tear' allowance called **depreciation** is included in the accounts.

— Credits on the revenue accounts —

Few items appear on the credit of either the trading or the profit and loss account. Generally, when they do, they often refer to small and miscellaneous profits and are usually taken to the lower account, and are identified by the words 'received' or 'recovered' as in the instances of discounts received, commissions received, rents received and bad debts recovered.

Bringing closing stocks into the books

When the new valuation figure for closing stock is credited to the trading account, a corresponding debit must be made on the stock account to sustain the full principles of double entry.

Since we are now reaching the final stage of the illustration commenced in Chapter 2, and the closing stock at 30 June has been valued at £80 and already taken to the credit of the trading account at the beginning of this chapter, we must now open a new stock account and debit this same amount to complete the double entry.

Dr.				Stock Account (20)				Cr.
June 30	Trading account		£ 80	00				

Pause for thought

- What is meant by the terms: revenue accounts, cost of sales, gross profit and net profit?
- Why is the main revenue account of the business split into two parts or sections.

Assignments

KEY POINTS

1 The heading of a revenue account should show the period covered and the date to which the account is made up.
2 Unless stated to the contrary, wages are normally taken to the trading account, and salaries to the profit and loss account. Some discretion should be used, as wages paid to office cleaners are chargeable to the lower account.
3 In the beginners' trial balances commencing stock is a debit, but closing stock (only just valued at the end of the period) *does not become a book entry until it is credited first to the trading account*.
4 Carriage inwards (on purchases, i.e. goods coming in) joins the purchase debit in the trading account, whereas carriage outwards (on sales, i.e. goods sent out) is a selling and delivery expense to be debited to the profit and loss account. *Both are debits*.
5 Neither assets (other than stocks) nor capital expenditure appear in revenue accounts.
6 Occasionally a business sustains a net loss. The effect on the trader's capital is explained in the next chapter.

7.1   Re-draft the statement below to show clearly the correct gross and net profit of this business.

Trade and Profit Account of Annabel Royle on 31 December

	£		£
Stock 31 Dec.	300	Sales	6200
Purchases	2850	Carriage	
Salaries	200	outwards	30
Gross profit c/d	3300	Stock 1 Dec.	420
	6650		6650
Carr. inwards	60	Gross profit	
Warehouse wages	1600	b/d	3300
Travelling	45		
Insurance	35		
Rent	80		
Drawings	100		
Net profit	1380		
	3300		3300

7.2 Extract the necessary information from this trial balance and make up the trading and profit and loss account of Wilfred Brazenbit, master plumber, for the month of June.

Trial Balance   30 June

	£	£
Capital W.B. 1 June		6 000
Drawings for month	400	
Van at valuation	1 750	
Office fittings at cost	350	
Purchases and sales	5 200	8 800
Carriage inwards	52	
Carriage outwards	46	
Advertising	108	
Insurance	30	
Petrol/oil	24	
Heating/lighting (workshop)	34	
Heating/lighting (office)	14	
Wages (workshop)	1 444	
Office salaries	420	
Stamps	8	
Stock 1 June	1 850	
Cash balance 30 June	3 070	
	14 800	14 800
Stock valuation at 30 June £2350		

Show the cost of the sales figure in the trading account of Mr Brazenbit.

8

THE BALANCE SHEET

The balance sheet takes care of the remaining 'open' balances in the books. After incorporating the retained profit (or loss) on trading, it depicts the assets, capital and liabilities at what should be their true or estimated net worth on a certain date.

The balance sheet *is not an account* but a financial statement, grouping and listing the business property and the capital and liabilities on that certain date. The date is important as the value of property, commodities, debts and obligations changes day by day.

Methods of presentation

This is the final stage of the illustration commenced in Chapter 2. First shown in the modern vertical style, which is now universally adopted, it would be presented in this way:

Balance Sheet as at 30 June

Assets employed		£	£	
Stock on hand	30 June	80.00		
Cash in hand		135.20	215.20	
Financed by				
Proprietor's capital	1 June	200.00		
Retained profit		15.20	215.20	

'Retained profit' is that balance of profit remaining after all appropriations (or withdrawals in the case of a sole trader) have been deducted.

If this vertical statement is tilted over to the right, the older horizontal 'T' style balance sheet is shown. Although this is no longer used, it is easier to follow double entry transactions in the horizontal presentations.

Balance Sheet as at 30 June

Capital and liabilities		£	Property and assets		£
Capital 1 June	£200.00		Stock 30 June	£80.00	
Add net profit	65.20		Cash in hand	135.20	215.20
	265.20				
Less drawings	50.00	215.20			
		215.20			215.20

Note that in horizontal presentation the proprietor's capital account is generally shown in fuller detail. In effect, it becomes a vertical copy of the owner's own personal ledger account (see page 42).

There should be no confusion between *debit* and *credit* at this stage. Double entry has already served its purpose and does not apply to the balance sheet. Again it is emphasised that the balance sheet is *not an account*, but a financial statement listing assets and liabilities at a certain date.

In this simple illustration there are only two assets and one liability at the balancing date, but even this small balance sheet has a story to tell. You started in business a month ago, made a small trading profit of £65.20, withdrew £50 on account of profits (thereby relinquishing part of your capital holding), and finally finished up with £15.20 more in asset value than when you started. Your capital or net worth at the end of the month of June is represented by the two assets, stock or merchandise not yet sold valued at £80.00, and £135.20 cash in hand; your net assets have thus increased by £15.20 since the beginning of June.

Net loss on trading

Occasionally a net loss might result through adverse or unfortunate trading conditions. The *debit balance* on the profit and loss account would be transferred to the *debit* of the proprietor's capital account in addition to personal drawings for the period. The net loss on trading would be reflected on the assets side of the balance sheet by a corresponding decrease in total net assets.

Capital and drawings

The capital account of the sole trader is an internal obligation of the business towards its owner, and must be kept quite distinct from the outside liabilities (trade and expense creditors to be introduced a little later). The business capital, now represented in the form of assets-in-trade, continues to finance the day-to-day trading operations of the business, but any withdrawals of money (or goods) for the private and family use of the proprietor involve a corresponding reduction of the capital account. Bear in mind, though, that we are in no way concerned how or in what manner the owner of a business disposes of the cash or the goods withdrawn in this way.

Closing of ledger accounts

In the exercise just completed, the proprietor's capital account is brought up to date by transferring the net profit (a credit balance of excess sales revenue) to the credit of that account, and also by transferring the debit balance on drawings account to the debit of capital account, as now shown:

Dr. **Drawings Account (4)** Cr.

			£					£	
June 30	Cash	CB1	50	00	June 30	Transfer to capital account	2	50	00

Capital Account (2)

			£					£	
June 30	Transfer from drawings account	4	50	00	June 1	Cash	CB1	200	00
30	Balance c/d		215	20		Net trading profit for month		65	20
			265	20				265	20
					July 1	Balance b/d		215	20

The recently created stock account remains open with its new debit balance of £80 at 30 June, but the remainder of the old revenue accounts is now *closed by transfer* to either the trading or profit and loss account.

Dr.   **Sales Account (15)**   Cr.

June 30	Transfer to trading account		£ 212	50	June 5 18 24	Cash Cash Cash	CB1 CB1 CB1	£ 45 56 110	80 20 50
			212	50				212	50

Purchases Account (5)

June 2 20	Cash Cash	CB1 CB1	£ 75 85	00 00	June 30	Transfer to trading account		£ 160	00
			160	00				160	00

Advertising Account (8)

June 12	Cash	CB1	£ 7	30	June 30	Transfer to P&L a/c		£ 7	30

Salaries Account (9)

June 30	Cash	CB1	£ 60	00	June 30	Transfer to P&L a/c		£ 60	00

Assignments

KEY POINTS

1 Assignment 8.1 is simple arithmetic. Remember, though, to add back drawings to the difference in capital values between the beginning and the end of the trading period. The sum withdrawn is part of the true profit made.

2 One main feature about vertical presentation of the balance sheet is that the figures take on more positive and realistic meaning, with the capital shown as representing the holding and value of net assets.

The vertical style balance sheet has superseded the old horizontal 'T' style in all forms of trading and professional firms in addition to limited companies.

The vertical style trading and profit and loss account has also become an accepted feature with most large organisations. For the time being, however, the revenue accounts will be presented in the older and more closely related two-sided accounts, probably easier to comprehend from a beginner's viewpoint with the similarity to the double entry ledger system itself.

3 In elementary book-keeping examinations, although arithmetical accuracy is important, even more important is the correct grouping and presentation of the figures, in particular on the balance sheet.

8.1 Davidia Kneale started in business a year ago with £5000 cash as capital. Her present capital, at 31 December, after one year's trading, cash transactions only, is represented by:

	£
Furniture/fittings	840
Stock of goods unsold	2680
Money in hand	3150

Miss Kneale has withdrawn £3180 on account of profits during the year. Can you work out her trading profit?

8.2 You are required to assemble Martin Kent's ledger balances (shown below) in trial balance form, with a view to finding out his opening capital.

In making out his final accounts for the month ended 31 May, show the cost of sales figure on his trading account.

	£
Stock 1 May	740
Purchases	3330
Sales	4650
Rent/rates proportion	136
Drawings	200
Salaries	400
Cash balance 31 May	1780
Insurance	12
Warehousing expense	30
Carriage inwards	7
Advertising	15

Martin Kent valued his closing stock at £530.

3.3 Enumerate some of the fixed and current assets you would expect
to see on the balance sheet of:
- (*a*) a small retail grocer
- (*b*) a village garage
- (*c*) an estate agent.

9

ILLUSTRATIVE EXAMPLE

As a basis for revision we take over the final balances shown on the balance sheet at 30 June in Chapter 8, and continue with a few further cash transactions for the month of July.

This means that we start the new period with the two debit balances of cash in hand £135.20 and stock £80.00, and one credit balance of £215.20, now our opening capital at 1 July.

As from the beginning of this new period our total debits equal our total credits. By simple equation $A = C + L$, where A is the symbol for the assets, C for the capital and L for the liabilities.

The trading transactions for the month of July are now listed.

July		£
2	Bought further goods to be re-sold	75.10
	Carriage on purchases	5.00
4	Cash sales	37.50
8	Paid for stationery	8.60
9	Cash sales	118.20
14	Bought new counter (*see text below*)	75.00
15	Received cash for goods sold	82.30
24	Cash sales	135.70
	Carriage on sales	2.00
	Paid for further purchases	54.00
25	Withdrew for family expenses	125.00
28	Paid salary to part-time assistant	86.00
30	Postages bought during month	8.00

The closing stock at 31 July was valued at £38.

Note that the transaction on 14 July is a special purchase of a *fixed asset*, bought for the permanent retention of the business and not for re-sale in the trading sense. The cost of this asset (£75) will be debited to a separate ledger account called the fittings account, to appear ultimately under its own heading on the assets side on the balance sheet at 31 July.

The various accounts are now written up.

Dr.   **Cash Account (2)**   Cr.

July			£		July			£	
1	Balance brought forward from June	CB1	135	20	2	Purchases	6	75	10
						Carriage inwards	17	5	00
4	Cash sales	16	37	50	8	Stationery	22	8	60
9	Cash sales	16	118	20	14	Fittings	3	75	00
15	Cash sales	16	82	30	24	Carriage outwards	18	2	00
24	Cash sales	16	135	70		Purchases	6	54	00
					25	Drawings	4	125	00
					28	Salaries	9	86	00
					30	Postages	24	8	00
					31	Balance c/d		70	20
			508	90				508	90
Aug. 1	Balance b/d		70	20					

It will be seen that the balance of cash in hand on 1 July is *only part of the business capital*, the part being invested in stock, as now depicted by the stock account as at 30 June brought forward.

Dr.   **Stock Account (20)**   Cr.

June 30	Trading account		£ 37	50					

The capital account is also brought forward to show clearly all the ledger accounts as from the beginning of the new period.

Dr.   **Capital Account (2)**   Cr.

					June 1	Balance b/f		£ 215	20

The remainder of the ledger accounts for the new period, to the completion stage of the double entry from the cash account, are now shown.

Dr.   **Purchases Account (6)**   Cr.

July			£					
2	Cash	CB2	75	10				
24	Cash	CB2	54	00				

Dr.   **Sales Account (16)**   Cr.

			July				£	
			4	Cash	CB2		37	50
			9	Cash	CB2		118	20
			15	Cash	CB2		82	30
			24	Cash	CB2		135	70
							373	70

Dr.   **Carriage Inwards (17)**   Cr.

July			£					
2	Cash	CB2	5	00				

Dr.   **Stationery (22)**   Cr.

July			£					
8	Cash	CB2	8	60				

Dr.   **Carriage Outwards (18)**   Cr.

July			£					
24	Cash	CB2	2	00				

Dr.   **Salaries (9)**   Cr.

July			£					
28	Cash	CB2	86	00				

Dr.   **Postages (24)**   Cr.

July			£					
30	Cash	CB2	8	00				

Dr.   **Drawings (24)**   Cr.

July			£					
25	Cash	CB2	125	00				

Dr.   **Fittings Account (3)**   Cr.

July			£					
14	Cash	CB2	75	00				

The postings have now been completed for the month of July. A trial balance will be taken out at this stage to prove the accuracy of the postings.

Trial Balance   31 July

	£	£
Cash in hand 31 July	70.20	
Capital 1 July		215.20
Drawings	125.00	
Fittings	75.00	
Purchases	129.10	
Sales		373.70
Carriage inwards	5.00	
Carriage outwards	2.00	
Stationery	8.60	
Salaries	86.00	
Postages	8.00	
Stock 1 July	80.00	
	588.90	588.90

Note that the opening stock at 1 July is debited to this general form of trial balance, but that the *closing stock of £38 at 31 July is not yet a balance in the books until the trading account is made up.*

All the revenue accounts for July are now closed (sales, purchases carriage inwards and outwards, stationery, salaries and postages) by transfer of their balances either to the trading account or to the profit and loss section of this combined revenue account.

Trading and Profit and Loss Account
for the month ended 31 July

	£		£
Stock 1 July	80.00	Sales for July	373.70
Purchases	129.10		
Carriage inwards	5.00		
	214.10		
Less stock 31 July	38.00		
Cost of sales	176.10		
Gross profit c/d	197.60		
	373.70		373.70
Carriage outwards	2.00	Gross profit b/d	197.60
Stationery	8.60		
Salaries	86.00		
Postages	8.00		
Net profit for July	93.00		
	197.60		197.60

The commencing stock at 1 July (£80.00) has now served its purpose by transfer of its debit balance to the trading account. That part of the stock account may now be ruled off. At this stage, too, the new valuation for closing at 31 July (£38.00) is *brought into the books for the first time by a credit to the trading account* (shown as a deduction on the debit side). The double entry and corresponding debit to stock account is now shown:

Dr.				Stock Account (20)			Cr.
June 30	Trading account	£ 80	00	July 31	Transfer of old stock to debit of trading a/c	£ 80	00
July 31	Trading a/c (new stock brought into books)	38	00				

At this final stage the assets are listed on the balance sheet in order of permanency, fittings being regarded as more permanent than stock, and stock thought to be rather more permanent than cash, with which it has been bought. The listing of the assets on order of permanency *as opposed to that of liquidity and realisation into cash* is simply a question of preference, generally followed by the majority of industrial, commercial and professional organisations, with big exceptions in the world of banking and finance whose huge enterprises like to display their formidable array of liquidity to the general public.

The balance sheet is now drawn up for the second month of the illustration started in Chapter 2. Note that the proprietor's equity and capital holding has decreased since 1 July by £32, the amount of the withdrawals in excess of the profit made during the month of July.

Balance Sheet as at 31 July

Assets employed		
Fixed assets		£
Fittings		75.00
Current assets		
Stock at 31 July	£38.00	
Cash in hand	70.20	108.20
		183.20
Financed by		
Capital 1 July	£215.20	
Add net profit	93.00	
	308.20	
Less drawings	125.00	183.20
		183.20

Assignment

CHECKPOINTS

Before starting Assignment 9.1, check yourself on the following routine, which, by this stage, should be becoming automatic.

1　Are your worked exercises reasonably neat and tidy, with the correct alignment of figures in the total columns?
2　Occasionally mistakes will occur. Instead of scratching out, simply rule through the error and insert the correct amount over the top.
3　Never rule free-hand. Always use a good ruler and keep any corresponding totals on the same horizontal level.
4　Are your headings clear and bold with a space for neatness between the ledger account heading and the details within the account?
5　Do you confine the use of the £ sign to the top of the amount column only, and write in the name of the month only at the top of the date column?

9.1　You start a part-time business on 1 January with an opening capital of £1500 comprising these assets:

	£
Second-hand fittings (counters and shelving) valued at	500
Stock of goods bought at the special price of	200
Available cash for business use	800
	1500

First record these details in your financial book as follows.

Debit £500 to fittings account ⎫ and credit £1500
Debit £200 to stock account ⎬ to your opening
Debit £800 to cash account ⎭ capital account.

Note that these three assets totalling £1500 make up your *commencing capital* in this instance. *The £800 cash is only part of your capital*.

After recording the opening entries, open the cash book and the ledger and post up the following transactions for the month of January. Take out a trial balance at 31 January, and make up the trading and profit and loss account and a balance sheet as at 31 January. The valuation of your closing stock is £375.

Jan.		£
2	Bought a second-hand van. Paid cash	650
	(debit van account – credit cash)	
3	Cash sales	162
	Bought stationery	8
	Paid rent for month	35
5	Bought goods for re-sale	188
	Cash takings	154
8	Paid fire/theft insurance (monthly payment)	25
	Cash sales	107
	Drew for 'self'	50
10	Paid part-time wages for warehousing	30
	(see note on wages in Chapter 7)	
	Travelling expenses of staff	14
	Bought a second-hand filing cabinet for office	85
14	Cash sales	76
16	Cash sales	166
	Paid wages	30
22	Paid for advertising	27
	Bought postage stamps	8
	Paid wages	30
23	Cash sales	148
	Further purchases to replenish stocks	155
	Paid carriage on goods bought	12
25	Cash sales	78
	Paid petrol account	22
	Repairs to van	24
	Cash purchases	186
28	Drew for 'self'	50
	Paid wages	30
31	Cash sales	72

Show as two distinct accounts, van account and fittings account, and debit the purchase of the filing cabinet (£85) to the latter. These *fixed asset* accounts are shown under their own headings at the top of the assets on the balance sheet.

10
CASH AND BANK TRANSACTIONS

All transactions up to this stage have been on a cash basis. Money has been received for cash sales, and all purchases and expenses of the business have been paid in cash, i.e. in currency notes and coin. Only a single-column type of cash account has been needed.

This may suit a small shop-keeper with sales across the counter for cash, but in most businesses these days there is a certain amount of credit dealing, and settlement by cheque or credit transfer has become both necessary and convenient.

The bank account

It has been emphasised that the cash account is part of the ledger system. It still remains an integral part of the old system, but with the introduction of banking facilities, a specially ruled ledger, called the **cash book**, now supersedes the former cash account.

The cash book has additional columns for bank transactions, and the two accounts for *both cash and bank* are balanced up independently. The account columns for cash and bank (cheques) are simply kept *side by side* for convenience, as quite often money (both cash and cheques) is paid out of the office cash surplus into the bank, and vice versa cash is withdrawn from the bank by cheque for the needs of the office.

Generally, both accounts have debit balances, but the bank account, unlike the cash account, could have a credit balance if the money at the bank was overdrawn. It would then be referred to as an **overdraft**.

In these early cash and bank exercises it is usual for the student to assume that cheques from customers are banked on the same day that they are received. In practice, however, the firm's cashier often pays all surplus cash together with customers' cheques into the business current account at the bank only once or twice a week.

An illustration is now shown of the two-column cash book. Note that the cash and bank columns are two separate accounts and are balanced up independently of each other. The bank columns in these early exercises relate entirely (on the debit side) to cheques received from customers and surplus cash paid into the bank and (on the credit side) to cheques drawn by the firm, withdrawing cash from the bank or in settlement of creditors' accounts.

Two-column Cash Book

Date			Cash	Bank	Date			Cash	Bank
Oct.			£	£	Oct.			£	£
1	Balance b/f		5.00	200.00	2	Contra	c		20.00
2	Contra	c	20.00		4	Rent			30.00
8	Cash sales		62.80		6	Purchases			88.50
12	L. Harris		22.70			Cleaning		12.50	
18	Cash sales		110.20		9	Stationery		4.80	
	Contra	c		100.00		Stamps		5.20	
22	P. Marsden Ltd			180.00	12	Purchases			66.60
28	Cash sales		82.50			Advertising			8.40
30	S. Roberts			78.90	16	T. Jones			42.30
31	Contra	c		150.00	18	Contra	c	100.00	
					19	Petrol/oil		8.20	
					24	Cleaning		12.50	
					28	G. Rawson & Son			55.50
					30	Salaries			185.00
					31	Contra	c	150.00	
						Drawings			55.00
						Balance c/d		10.00	157.60
			303.20	708.90				303.20	708.90
Nov.									
1	Balances b/d		10.00	157.60					

The small letter 'c' in the folio columns indicates **contra** entries, or transfers between office cash and bank and vice versa. These postings, shown on both sides of the cash book, debit in one column for the corresponding credit on the other side, cancel themselves out, so that *ledger postings are unnecessary*.

Any charges made by the bank (interest on overdrafts etc.) are shown as deductions on the bank statement sent to the customer at the end of the month, or sometimes quarterly. The firm's cashier, on checking the bank statement against the company's cash book bank columns, will enter any bank charges of this nature on the *credit side* of the cash book bank column. Later the ledger clerk will complete the double entry by posting the amount to the *debit* of the bank charges account in the nominal or expense ledger.

Cash or cheque?

Sometimes, in an examination question, it may not be clear whether a receipt or a payment is to be entered in the cash or the bank column. In the absence of instructions, make it a rule to treat all payments from customers, and all payments to suppliers, as *cheque payments*, since cash would not be sent through the post. On the other hand, the purchase of a pint of milk for the coffee, payment of a few pounds to a window cleaner, etc. are probably made in cash. Remember, too, that postages and parcels taken to the Post Office are usually paid in cash.

The important thing is to avoid the complication of an overdrawn cash balance which, strictly, should not be possible. *When in doubt, pay by cheque.*

Primary records

The entries on the debit side of the cash book originate from the daily till rolls of cash registers, duplicate receipt books and from the listed amounts on the bank paying-in slips.

Entries on the credit side of the cash book originate from the official receipts from suppliers, cash memos from sundry small purchases, and the counterfoil stubs of the firm's cheque books.

Assignments

KEY POINTS

1 Check the contra items to ensure that there is a debit to correspond with every credit. Do not guess with regard to contras. Think which account has increased or received benefit (cash or bank?). Debit cash and credit bank or vice versa as the case may be.

2 Generally there are more items and lengthier columns to add up in the firm's cash book. The importance of correct alignment cannot be over-emphasised.

3 Usually there are more entries on the credit or payments side of the cash book. This means leaving a few blank spaces on the debit, when balancing up, as the totals must be on the same horizontal. Remember, too, that allowance must be made on the credit side of the cash columns (and generally bank columns too) for the cash and bank balances.

4 Where personal names are given (the names of people and firms), these names should be recorded in the details column of the cash book. Generally the receipt or payment refers to the settlement of a credit account already posted up from an original invoice to a customer's or supplier's ledger account.

5 It is not necessary to record the names of suppliers or customers *where goods are bought or sold for cash or cheque payment* at the time the goods are handed over in completion of the transaction, i.e. cash sales and cash purchases transactions.

10.1 Enter the following cash and cheque transactions in a two-column cash book for the month of April, balancing up both cash and bank columns at 30 April.

April		£
1	Cash in office	40.00
	Cash at bank	560.00
3	Cash sales	56.28
	Paid cash into bank	50.00
	Paid rent by cheque	35.00
8	Paid Jim Lord by cheque	28.40
	Cash purchases	12.70
14	Cheque from R. Davies	25.60
	Cash sales	54.84
	Cash paid into bank	50.00
18	Bought stamps	3.00
	Drew cheque for 'self'	60.00
25	Paid Ossie Pye by cheque	48.80
30	Bought some shelving from A.B.C Services Ltd	36.30

10.2 On 1 September Charmain Wade's cash and bank balances were £10 and £640. Her transactions during the month are listed below. Write up her cash book for September, bringing down her cash and bank balances as at 1 October.

Sept.		£
1	Cheque drawn for office cash	40.00
3	Bought goods from Bob West	80.00
5	Paid Sam Ronson's account	24.20
	Paid office cleaner (cash)	18.00
8	Cash sales	78.80
	Paid cash into bank	50.00
12	Bought stamps	3.00
	Paid rates by cheque	135.50
15	Cash sales	68.70
18	Cash sales	72.30
	Paid wages out of cash	55.00
	Drew cheque for 'self'	80.00
22	Paid Josh Brown's account	36.40
	Leslie Frost paid by cheque	66.60
24	Cash sales	94.90
	Paid cash into bank	50.00
26	Cash purchases	15.20
	Paid wages	55.00
	Bought stamps	5.00
27	Paid advertising account	22.50
29	Sarah Raven sent cheque in payment of old account	25.00
30	Miss Wade paid all surplus cash over £10 into the bank	

11

BANK RECONCILIATION

In this chapter we concern ourselves solely with the bank columns of the cash book and the agreement or reconciliation of these columns with the bank's own statement forwarded monthly, or to bank customers on request.

It is seldom that the bank balance according to the cash book agrees with the balance according to the bank's own statement on the same date. This is due to the time lag between the receipt of cheques from the firm's customers, and their actual settlement or collection from the bank accounts of the debtors. Again, there is a similar delay between the handing over or posting of cheques drawn in favour of the suppliers or creditors, and their collection, via their bankers, from the account of the paying firm.

—— Checking the bank statement ——

Apart from the delay in clearing, presenting and collection of cheques, there are often other bank debits for charges and expenses that appear periodically on the bank statement. Instances of these are the interest charged by the bank on loans and overdrafts, and sometimes charges per cheque drawn. Often there will be payments out that have been made as direct debits or standing orders in compliance with the instructions of the customer. Equally, the business may have received standing orders or direct debits. It is also increasingly common for bills to be met by direct transfer between bank accounts using the BACS or CHAPS systems.

Dividends from investments owned by the business are often paid direct to the bank, and it is only when credited to the firm's current account and checked through reconciliation by the cashier that these amounts will be entered in the cash book. The cash book in this way is brought up to date as far as possible before the final reconciliation takes place, which involves ticking, item for item, all the debits in the cash book against all the credits on the bank statement, and all the credits in the cash book against all the debits on the bank statement.

A note is made of *all amounts remaining unticked* in either the cash book or the bank statement. It is these unticked items which form the basis for the reconciliation.

Cash Book (bank columns only)

Dr.   Cr.

June		Cash £	Bank £	June		Cash £	Bank £
1	Balance b/f	✓	300.00	2	Cheque to X	✓	16.20
8	Cash paid in	✓	70.20	5	Rates	✓	44.00
10	Cheque from A	✓	24.50	12	Wages	✓	60.00
15	Cheque from B	✓	36.30	15	Advertising		8.50
25	Cash banked	✓	66.10	24	Wages	✓	60.00
28	Cheque from C		55.50	28	Cheque to Y		9.70
				30	Cheque to Z		36.40
					Balance c/d		317.80
			552.60				552.60
July 1	Balance b/d		317.80				

Bank Statement

June		Debit £	Credit £	Balance £
1	Balance b/f			✓ 300.00
4	X	✓ 16.20		283.80
8	Cash receipts		✓ 70.20	354.00
9	Rates	✓ 44.00		310.00
12	Wages	✓ 60.00		250.00
	A		✓ 24.50	274.50
18	B		✓ 36.30	310.80
19	Chq. no. 22643	✓ 8.50		302.30
24	Wages	✓ 60.00		242.30
25	Cash receipts		✓ 66.10	308.40
28	TS dividend		50.00	358.40
	Standing order	10.50		347.90
30	Charges	4.00		343.90

—— Procedure for reconciliation ——

Note that all items in the firm's cash book have been ticked off with the exception of:

- C's cheque for £55.50 not yet cleared by the bank
- the cheques made out to Y and Z for £9.70 and £36.40 not yet presented for payment.

All items on the bank statement have been ticked off except for the debits against the firm for £10.50 and £4.00, and the dividend of £50 paid direct to the bank.

The firm's cashier now brings the company cash book up to date as far as possible, to show an *amended bank balance* of £353.30 thus:

Dr.				**Cash Book** (continuation)			Cr.
			£				£
June 30	Balance b/f		317.80	June 30	Standing order		10.50
	Treasury stock div.				Bank charges		4.00
	Paid direct to bank		50.00		Balance c/d		353.30
			367.80				367.80
July 1	Balance b/d		353.30				

The cheque not yet cleared and the cheques not yet presented for payment are adjusted on the reconciliation statement as follows.

Bank Reconciliation Statement   30 June

		£	£
Amended balance as per cash book			353.30
Add cheques drawn but not yet presented for payment	Y	9.70	
	Z	36.40	46.10
			399.40
Deduct cheque not yet cleared (i.e. not yet credited to the firm's current account)			55.50
Balance according to bank statement			343.90

Assignments

KEY POINTS

1   You will probably comprehend, at this stage, that a 'debit' bank balance in the firm's cash book means that there is money (perhaps a fairly adequate reserve) at the bank.

From the bank's accounting aspect, however, you are *in credit*, i.e. the bank owes you money.

When you pay cash and cheques into your bank account, your current account is credited, thereby increasing your bank balance; but when you withdraw money or make a payment by cheque, your bank current account is debited, thereby reducing your bank balance.

2   'Cheques not presented yet for payment' are those cheques given or sent to creditors who have not yet claimed or collected payment from your bank.

'Cheques and cash not yet cleared' refers to remittances (currency and cheques) paid into your own bank, but not yet shown on your bank statement. Often this is the total of the last paying-in slip handed in to the bank on the last day of the month.

3   The reverse of the conventional procedure applies when dealing with a bank overdraft, your bank account perhaps temporarily being 'in the red'.

Cash and cheques paid into the account reduce the overdraft, whereas further cheques drawn increase it.

4   The correct figure for the business bank balance to be taken to the trial balance and also to the balance sheet is always the *adjusted or amended figure according to the cash book*.

11.1   The cash book bank balance of Alan Jones on 30 June shows a debit balance of £728.24, whereas the statement given to him by his bank on the same date shows a credit balance in his favour of £696.93.

Checking the bank statement against his cash book, Mr Jones finds that cash and cheques paid into his bank on 30 June, totalling £224.75, had not been credited to his current account; and two cheques for £82.64 and £110.80 sent to Holt Bros Ltd and Eric Hardwick on 28 June had not yet been presented to his bank for payment.

You are required to draw up a reconciliation statement showing the difference between the two balances mentioned in the first paragraph above.

11.2   The bank statement of Linda Owen made up to 31 December, received early in the New Year, showed her current account overdrawn by £24.54.

Checking the statement against the bank columns of her cash book, she noted the following.

(a)   Cash and cheques totalling £178.28 paid into the bank on 31 December had not been credited to her account.

(b)   A cheque for £83.40 sent to her supplier on 29 December had not yet been presented for payment.

(c)   A dividend of £60 Treasury Stock had been credited direct to her account.

(d)   Bank charges of £12.50 had been debited to her account by the bank.

What was the bank balance shown by Miss Owen's cash book on 31 December?

12
THE PETTY CASH BOOK

Under what is known as the **imprest system** of keeping petty cash, a round sum of money (say £20) is handed over to a junior clerk or typist, who becomes responsible for the payment of small expenses of the office.

At the end of the week or the month, the *exact amount of money paid out* (the **total disbursements**) is refunded by the main cashier to the petty cashier, so that the balance of petty cash in hand is brought back again to the original amount of the imprest, i.e. £20.

An analysis cash book, with columns specially ruled to suit the needs of the particular office and the general expense payments, is used for this purpose of relieving the main cashier of some of the routine work. This book is called the **petty cash book**.

Posting of the petty cash expense totals

The petty cash book is part of the double entry system because the imprest amount is transferred from the credit of the main cash book to the petty cashier. The totals of the various expense columns of the petty cash book are extracted and debited to the relative expense accounts in the nominal ledger, and at the end of the trading period the balance of petty cash in hand is included or absorbed into the main cash balance.

Illustration

A simple style of petty cash ruling is shown below with analysis columns for four classes of routine expense. The commencing balance of petty cash on hand, the imprest amount, at the beginning of the month of January is £20. The expense payments are listed for the first week of the New Year, and this page of the petty cash book balanced up on 6 January.

Disbursements for the first week of January:

Jan.		£
1	Paid bus fare	0.68
2	Bought postage stamps	2.00
	Paid for office cleaning	4.00
3	Bought coffee	1.64
4	Paid for pencils	0.76
	Bought more stamps	1.00
5	Taxi fare to station	2.25
	Donation to Oxfam	1.00
6	String	0.65

Petty Cash Book

Rec'd from cashier	Date	Details of expense	Voucher no.	Total	Stamps Stat'y	Travel	Cleaning	Sundries
£	Jan.			£	£	£	£	£
20.00	1	Imprest b/f						
	1	Bus fares	–	0.68		0.68		
	2	Stamps	1	2.00	2.00			
		Cleaning	2	4.00			4.00	
	3	Coffee	3	1.64				1.64
	4	Pencils	4	0.76	0.76			
		Stamps	5	1.00	1.00			
	5	Taxi fare	–	2.25		2.25		
		Oxfam donation	6	1.00				1.00
	6	String	7	0.65				0.65
				13.98	3.76	2.93	4.00	3.29
	6	Balance c/d		6.02				
20.00				20.00				
6.02	8	Balance b/d						
13.98	8	Imprest refund						

Note that each item of expense in the petty cash book is shown both in the total column and in the appropriate analysis column. The totals of the combined analysis columns agree with the sum of the main total column (£13.98). This is the total petty cash expenditure for the week, and, when deducted from the original imprest amount of £20.00, leaves a balance of £6.02 petty cash in hand at 6 January.

At the end of the week the main cashier will refund to the petty cashier the sum of £13.98 (the total disbursements) so that the balance of the imprest for the commencement of the second week is made up to the original sum of £20.00.

As far as possible, vouchers and receipts for payment of these small expenses should be asked for, so that they can be verified by the main cashier. It should be possible to obtain a receipt from the cleaner, and the Post Office counter clerk will date stamp a petty cash disbursement slip when stamps are bought.

Assignments

KEY POINTS

1   The word 'imprest' means loan. The imprest amount is loaned or advanced by the main cashier to the petty cashier.

2   The analysis columns in use refer to regular routine expenses, often office expenses.

   A 'sundries' or 'miscellaneous' column takes care of casual and incidental expenses.

3   Sometimes an extra column is brought into use for the payment of small and occasional payments to a few creditors' accounts in the bought (suppliers) ledger.

4   Where a full length exercise includes a petty cash book, remember to bring the petty cash balance on to the trial balance at the close of the trading period, and again on the assets side of the balance sheet.

5   Remember, too, that all the *analysis expense totals* must be taken to the *debit of* nominal ledger accounts, and brought to the debit of the trial balance. This would not apply, though, to the settlement of small bought ledger accounts (see KP3 above).

12.1 Willie Woodbine is the petty cashier of a small textile manufacturer. He is responsible for a weekly imprest of £30. During his absence on holiday, you are required to write up his petty cash book for the first week of March, using four analysis expense columns. Show the amount of the imprest refund at the end of the week.

March		£
1	Petty cash imprest in hand	30.00
	Bought stamps	3.00
2	Paid for travelling	3.20
	Milk for office	0.82
3	Newspapers	0.65
	Fax roll	2.50
4	Bought stamps	3.00
	Paid bus fare	1.28
	Donation to charity	0.50
5	Wrapping paper and string	1.48

12.2 Rule up a petty cash book with five analysis columns and enter the routine expenses shown below. Show the imprest refund at the end of the first week in May.

May

1 Petty cash in hand £35
2 Bought stamps £4; paid £3.85 for stationery; and 75p for tea and milk.
3 Paid cleaner £5; 52p excess postage due and £2.50 taxi fare for a sick employee.
4 Bought £4 stamps; refunded 36p bus fare to newly engaged typist.
5 Window cleaner £2.35; fax roll £2.26; donation to police charity £2.

12.3 Explain what is meant by 'petty cash imprest'.

Rule up a petty cash book with four analysis columns and with an imprest of £50. Make up your own headings and expense details for two weeks, balance up, and show the imprest refund.

13

CREDIT TRANSACTIONS AND SUPPLIERS' ACCOUNTS

All trading transactions, up to this stage, have been on a cash (or cheque) immediate payment basis. Modern business, however, is built upon credit, buying and obtaining the possession and use of the goods or services today, but delaying the payment and settlement for a few weeks or even a month or two. This means that permanent records must be kept of these credit transactions, and also of debtors and creditors.

A debtor is a customer who has bought goods or obtained a service *on credit*, i.e. the goods or the services received have not been paid for yet. *Money is owed by a debtor*.

A creditor, in the business sense, is the supplier of goods or services, who has not yet been paid. *Money is owing to a creditor*.

Day books or journals

Subsidiary books called **day books** or **journals** are used for the initiation of credit transactions in connection with the purchase and sale of merchandise on credit. These books, referred to as **original records of entry**, are used as aids for posting the ledger accounts. Generally, after the extraction of essential information the books are stored away, to be produced for checking by the firm's auditor when required.

An illustration is now given of this new procedure as applied to the purchases side of the business and the trade creditors' accounts.

The purchases day book

The primary accounting document for merchandise bought on credit is the supplier's bill or **invoice**, handed over to the purchaser by the vendor at the time of the purchase or sent to the purchaser's address by post.

An invoice is shown first, the essential information then being extracted from it and posted to part of a folio of the purchases day book, or **bought journal** as it is sometimes called.

Samuel Smith South Parade Seatown	**INVOICE** **BOUGHT OF DAVID BROWN** **5 Eastgate Stafford**		No. 876 3 Feb. 19..	
Stock Ref.		£		£
Y 38	½ doz. white cotton vests			
	size 16 @ £3.60	21 60		
	Less 25% trade discount	5 40	16 20	
P 54	3 doz. pair Nustyle			
	socks @ £1	36 00		
	Less 20% trade discount	7 20	28 80	
	E.&O.E.	Net	45 00	

The ruling of the purchases day book is similar to that of the journal, the exercise book generally used by students for trial balances.

Purchases Day Book (36)

Feb. 3	Invoices from suppliers David Brown Stafford	BL 52			£ 45 00

The postings from another three invoices are now added to the **purchases day book** (PDB), to allow the illustration of the double entry procedure between the day book and the personal and nominal ledger accounts:

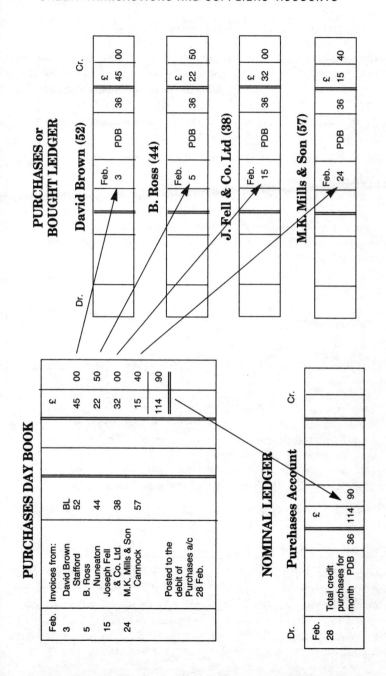

PURCHASES DAY BOOK

Feb.	Invoices from:			£	
3	David Brown Stafford	BL	52	45	00
5	B. Ross Nuneaton		44	22	50
15	Joseph Fell & Co. Ltd		38	32	00
24	M.K. Mills & Son Cannock		57	15	40
				114	90

Posted to the
debit of
Purchases a/c
28 Feb.

PURCHASES or BOUGHT LEDGER

Dr. **Cr.**

David Brown (52)

| Feb. 3 | | PDB | 36 | £ 45 | 00 |

B. Ross (44)

| Feb. 5 | | PDB | 36 | £ 22 | 50 |

J. Fell & Co. Ltd (38)

| Feb. 15 | | PDB | 36 | £ 32 | 00 |

M.K. Mills & Son (57)

| Feb. 24 | | PDB | 36 | £ 15 | 40 |

NOMINAL LEDGER

Purchases Account

Dr. **Cr.**

| Feb. 28 | Total credit purchases for month | PDB | 36 | £ 114 | 90 |

— 69 —

Each invoice is certified and approved for payment before being entered in the purchases day book. The details on the invoice are checked against the daily records of goods received by the receipts store manager, who initials the debit note prior to its approval for payment by the buying office. After the price and the correctness of the trade discount has been confirmed, the only essential to be recorded in the day book is the date of the invoice, its official number, the name of the supplier and the net amount to be paid.

Where value added tax is applicable, separate columns are needed in the day book. This is explained in Chapter 16.

The purchases day book is used for goods bought on credit for re-sale, or for re-sale after conversion. *Permanent assets acquired such as fittings and office equipment are not posted in the day book*: if these are bought on credit, they are debited direct to the asset account and credited to the personal account of the supplier.

Cash purchases (which may also be paid for by cheque) are taken direct from the credit of the cash book to the debit of a separate nominal ledger account, and the cash memo details are filed in a separate folder for easy access by the auditor.

Trade discount

Trade discount is a special trade allowance generally recognised between firms within the same trade or industry, and operating between manufacturers, wholesalers and retailers. The discount is normally a percentage ranging between 10 and 35%, and is always deducted from the supplier's invoice. *Only the net amount of the invoice is posted to the day book and to the creditor's account.*

Trade discount is not recorded in any account under its own heading.

Cash discount and the three-column cash book

Cash discount is generally a far smaller allowance, offered as an inducement to the prompt payment of the accounts of credit customers. There is no reason, though, why cash discounts should not be offered in the form of a **spot** or **net price** to cash customers, but in this instance the discount would not be recorded as part of the cash sale, which would simply be shown at its reduced price.

To operate a cash discount, a **three-column cash book** is required, showing discount as well as cash and bank. Cash discount is entered in the discount column of the cash book on the left of the payment to which it relates, and the combined total of the *money paid plus the cash discount* allowed or received is posted to the personal account of the credit customer or the supplier of the merchandise.

Purchases account

The same purchases account is used for both cash and credit purchases, but now there is a slight change of procedure for credit purchases. The individual debits (invoice totals) are not posted to the nominal ledger at the time they are entered in the day book, but are allowed to accumulate day by day and are *posted in one total for the month* to the purchases account at the end of each month.

The individual supplier's (creditor's) account, however, is posted up immediately, direct from the day book, so that at any time the amount owing to any creditor may quickly be ascertained.

Creditor's accounts

The balances outstanding (unpaid) on all suppliers' accounts are listed at the end of the trading period. The total for 'trade creditors' is taken to the credit side of the trial balance, its final destination being under the heading of current liabilities on the balance sheet.

Payments made to creditors in settlement of their accounts *in no way affect the purchases total* on the debit of purchases account.

Cash or credit?

Students sometimes experience a little difficulty in deciding whether a transaction is for cash or on credit. These rules will help.

- Unless instructed to the contrary, assume that all transactions for the purchase or the sale of goods are on credit when a personal name or the name of a firm is mentioned in the question. There should be no need to mention the name of the buyer or vendor in

the cash of a cash purchase or a cash sale as money is simply exchanged for the goods handed over.
- Assets and office equipment are often bought on credit, and again this should be assumed when the name of the supplier is mentioned, but remember that the cost of the asset should be credited direct to the supplier's account and the debit taken direct to the asset account.
- Cash purchases, cash sales and all transactions where the word 'paid' is mentioned are obviously cash transactions.

The buyer's records

Accounting systems and rulings vary a good deal, but the general principles involved in the purchase and sale of goods remains basically the same. On the purchase side, illustrated opposite, start with the official order placed with the supplier and follow through (a) the initiation of the storehouse procedure, and then (b) invoicing process and the various aspects of documentation.

DOCUMENTS AND ACCOUNT BOOKS

Pause for thought

- What is a book of prime or original entry? Does the cash book fall into this category?
- What kind of purchases are entered up in the bought journal?
- Would you expect to find the purchase of a new car posted to the bought journal? If not, how would you deal with this acquisition?
- What is another name for the bought journal?

Assignments

KEY POINTS

1 Money is owing to trade creditors. Their ledger accounts kept in the bought ledger, for merchandise supplied on credit, have not yet been paid.

2 The purchases or bought day book is a book of prime entry, used for recording invoices of credit purchases (goods to be re-sold or material bought with a view to reconditioning it for sale). Other books of prime entry are the cash book, the sales day book and the returns books.

3 Suppliers' accounts, kept in the bought ledger, have credit balances. The individual credits have been posted to these accounts day by day from the bought day book. The day book totals are carried forward until the end of the month, and then the monthly total is taken to the debit side of the purchases account in the nominal ledger, thus completing the double entry.

4 Trade discount is an allowance made from the vendor's price list or catalogue. the deduction is made from the invoice and the net amount due to the creditor is posted *net* to the credit of the supplier's account in the bought ledger.

5 Payments made to the creditors in no way affect the day book or the total taken to purchases account. These payments concern only the cash book and the personal accounts of creditors.

13.1 Enter up the bought day book of Maree Lyritis from the details below, and post up the double entry to the bought ledger.

July

4   Bought £80 of goods from Adrian Shaw less 20% trade discount.

9   Received delivery of £28.50 goods from Samuel Swift. This included £2.50 transport costs.

18   Bought another £60 of goods from Adrian Shaw less usual T.D.

24   Ordered by telephone £45 of goods from W.H.T. Suppliers Ltd. Forwarded and invoiced the following day.

30   Received a debit note for £18 from Samuel Swift for goods delivered and checked the previous day.

Assuming Miss Lyritis settled the two earlier accounts of Shaw and Swift on 20 July, show all ledger accounts in full detail and balance up on 31 July.

13.2   Garry Hall commenced trading with £800 in the bank and a stock of goods valued at £200 on 1 April. His transactions during April are listed below.

April		£
2	Cashed cheque for office	50.00
	Bought goods from Tom Wynne £60 (gross) arranging for trade discount of 25% on all purchases	
4	Cash sales	126.30
	Paid for stationery (cash)	8.40
	Bought stamps	4.00
6	Bought goods from Fred Maples	36.60
	Cash sales	156.80
	Paid cash into bank	200.00
	Bought goods from Wynne (gross)	80.00
12	Paid Maples on account	20.00
	Paid insurance	15.50
	Sent cheque for advertising	12.20
18	Cash sales	162.70
	Paid into bank	100.00
	Cash purchases (cheques)	18.25
	Paid Wynne's April account	105.00
30	Cheque for month's wages	320.00
	Cash for 'self'	60.00

Post all transactions through original records to the ledger accounts. Balance all accounts and take out a trial balance at 30 April.

14

THE ACCOUNTS OF CREDIT CUSTOMERS

When merchandise is sold on credit, the ownership of the goods passes immediately to the buyer who, at the time of the purchase or perhaps a few days later, receives an invoice from the vendor showing the full details of the sale, with trade discount deducted if this is applicable, and the net amount to be paid in due course

Sales day book

In the books of the vendor, credit sales follow a similar procedure to that already outlined on the purchase side in the previous chapter, another book of original entry being brought into use called the sales day book (abbreviation SDB).

Before computerisation, the larger organisations, most of them on fully mechanised accounting, made several copies of each invoice sent to their credit customers, one copy being taken by the accounts department and used for making up the sales day book, which again, like the purchase day book, served as an aid towards the accuracy and mechanical efficiency of modern accounting methods.

The essential details (date, name of customer, and net amount) were taken from the copy of the invoice sent to the credit customer and entered in the sales day book, trade discount being deducted (if allowable) to show the net charge to the customer. Only this *net amount* was posted to the debit of the customer's sales ledger account.

The daily sales total was carried forward and at the end of the month the total gross sales were credited to sales account in the nominal ledger. The illustration shows the posting procedure between the day book and the personal and nominal ledgers.

Illustration   The posting procedure between day book and ledgers

SALES or DEBTORS' LEDGER

R. Young (23)

Dr.				£		Cr.
Feb. 5	SDB	28		18	80	

E. Harper & Co. (32)

Feb.				£		
12	SDB	28		48	00	

Stanley Wood (Hale) Ltd (37)

Feb.				£		
20	SDB	28		29	20	

Leslie Steel (43)

Feb.				£		
25	SDB	28		36	60	

SALES DAY BOOK

Feb.	Invoices sent to:	SL		£	
5	R. Young	23		18	80
12	E. Harper & Co.	32		48	00
20	Stanley Wood (Hale) Ltd	37		29	20
25	Leslie Steel Repton	43		36	60
				132	60
	Posted to the credit of Sales Account 28 Feb. NL	20			

NOMINAL LEDGER

Sales Account (20)

Dr.						Cr. £
			Feb. 28	Total credit sales for month SDB	28	132 60

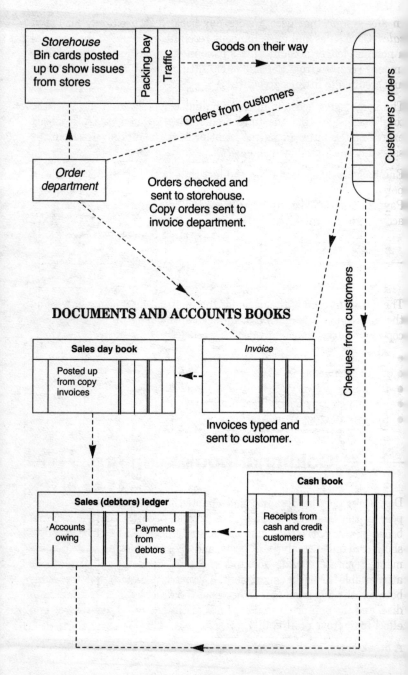

DOCUMENTS AND ACCOUNTS BOOKS

n any system that uses a sales day book, it is used only for *credit* *sales*. Cash sales and miscellaneous receipts are taken to the credit of a nominal ledger account unless in connection with the sale of assets money received from the sale of old fittings would be debited to cash and credited to fittings account).

The same sales account in the nominal ledger is used for both the total cash sales and the total credit sales, in elementary textbook exercises, the latter being the transfer of the monthly total from the sales day book, as shown on page 77.

Emphasis is again laid upon the fact that payments in settlement of personal accounts *in no way affect the monthly total of sales*. Payments by debtors simply involve the cash book and the personal accounts of the credit customers.

The sales records

The **copy invoice** is the basis for the financial accounting entries on the sales side of the business. In mechanised accounting at least five copies of the customer's invoice are needed for processing:

- the original to the credit customer (the debtor)
- a sales department copy
- the advice/delivery note (without financial detail)
- a despatch copy for traffic office
- the accounts departmental copy.

Columnar book-keeping

Day books may be designed and adapted to suit the needs and purpose of the business. If there are several departments the original books of entry for credit purchases and credit sales can be ruled to show a detailed analysis of costs and the revenue for each department. Separate trading accounts can then be made up, with stocks attributable to each department. Comparisons may then be made between the departments, or between the different lines of merchandise, and the non-profit making lines discarded, or economies put into effect to improve profitability.

A break-down of the merchanting costs on the purchase side of a business with three separate departments might take the following form, in so far as the bought journal is concerned (VAT is ignored for ease of comprehension).

Date	Supplier	Inv. No.	BL folio	Total	Dept. X	Dept. Y	Dept. Z
June				£	£	£	£
1	S. Adams	36	24	120	55	65	–
3	L.H. Dale	45	16	14			14
	Guy Lord	46	176	240	150	40	50
6	Jay & Lee	47	82	72		48	24

Assignments

KEY POINTS

1 Money is owing by debtors. The listed total for trade debtors is taken to the debit of the trial balance and shown under the heading of 'current assets' on the balance sheet.

2 Brief details are taken from copies of the invoices sent to customers, to make up the sales day book.
Some firms make up the spare copies of customers' invoices into book form, and this becomes their day book, the daily totals being carried forward and at the end of the month these accumulated totals are posted in one big total to the credit of sales account.

3 Neither the sales day book nor the sales account are affected by the individual payments from debtors, the accounting entries involved simply concerning only the cash book and the customer's personal ledger account in the sales or debtors' ledger.

14.1 What is another name for the sales day book?
What kind of sales are posted to the sales day book? How would you deal with daily cash sales across the counter? Which books or records are indicated by these abbreviations?
PDB   SDB   BJ   PCB   BL   SL

14.2 Felicity Jones commenced business on 1 October with £500 in the bank and a stock of goods valued at £200. These are her recorded transactions for the month of October.

Oct.		£
1	Cashed cheque for the office	50.00
	Ordered £40 of goods from Sarah Gosling subject to 20% trade discount. The merchandise was delivered the next day.	
3	General expenses paid in cash	6.00
	Paid for some advertising by cheque	15.50
	Cash sales	72.40
9	Cash purchases	9.10
	Cheque drawn for 'self'	30.00
12	Cash sales	87.20
	Paid cash into bank	100.00
	Sold goods (on credit) to Tom Lister	25.80
15	Bought £60 of goods from Roy Morris less 10%, and sold £45 of goods to Ted Batten making him an allowance also of 10%	
18	Cash sales	66.70
	Paid Sarah Gosling's account	
20	Received cheque from Tom Lister	25.80
	Sold £30 of goods to Ted Batten, invoiced gross less10%	
25	Drew cheque to pay salary of part-time receptionist	90.00
	Withdrew cash for private use	50.00
30	Cash sales	58.60
31	Paid all surplus cash into bank except for a cash float of £20	

You are required to post up all the original records, balance up all ledger accounts, and take out a trial balance on 31 October.

15
PURCHASES AND SALES RETURNS

Goods are returned to suppliers for a variety of reasons. They may have been damaged in transit; they may not be what was ordered; the wrong size or another colour may have been consigned in error.

Credit note

The vendor (the supplier) will be expected to make an allowance or rebate from the amount on the original invoice, where certain merchandise is returned. This allowance applies also when returnable crates, packages and containers are sent back to the supplier.

The vendor's document agreeing or certifying the rebate is called a **credit note**. It is similar to the invoice but is normally printed or written in red to distinguish it from the debit note (the invoice).

Accounting for returns

The accounting procedure is not complicated. It simply involves putting the whole or part of the original transaction in reverse. When goods are returned to your supplier, your *total purchases are thereby reduced*, and, if bought on credit, you do *not owe your creditor so much*. The original transaction or part of it is reversed by debiting your supplier's account and crediting purchases with the value of the goods returned.

Similarly on the sales side. When the credit customer returns some goods to the supplier, the figure for the *recorded sales is reduced* (in the books of the vendor) and the *debtor does not owe so much*. The book-keeping procedure is a debit to sales account and a credit to the personal account of the customer (debtor) for the value of the goods returned.

One important thing to remember about the return of goods is that any **trade discount** deducted on the original purchase or sale must also apply and be *deducted from the gross value* of the goods which are returned.

In practice, when a trader's returns of goods sold are few and infrequent, brief details of the returns are often recorded at the back of the ordinary purchases and sales day books.

In the larger firms, and particularly where returns are more numerous, separate returns day books are brought into operation. These are known as the **returns outwards book (purchase returns)** and the **returns inwards book (sales returns)**.

The ultimate destination of the returns is to the credit of the purchases account or the debit of the sales account, but in the meantime the trial balance may be made up. Assuming that the returns have already been taken in reduction of purchases and sales account, the *net purchases* and the *net sales* figures are debited and credited to the trial balance, but it would not be incorrect to show the gross figures for the purchases and the sales together with separate amounts for the returns, i.e. a debit for returns inwards (sales returns) and a credit for returns outwards (purchase returns).

Illustration

Let us assume that two of the white cotton vests invoiced by David Brown on 3 February (Chapter 13) were torn in transit, and that a claim is made by the buyer Samuel Smith against the full charge shown on the original invoice no. 876 dated 3 February.

David Brown would investigate his customer's complaint and examine the faulty merchandise. He acknowledges the claim by sending a credit note, say on 8 February, to Samuel Smith, for the value of the two vests already charged, i.e. £7.20 *less trade discount* at 25% which was deducted from the original invoice.

In Samuel Smith's books (the purchaser's books) the posting from the returns outwards book to the creditor's bought ledger account is shown, which reduces the balance due to this supplier by £5.40. The purchases account total for the month is also reduced by the same amount by a credit for these returns which is posted from the returns outwards book at the end of February.

In the illustration shown, the returns outwards book total for February has been taken direct to the credit of purchases account at the end of the month. In some instances an account might be opened for these purchase returns called purchase returns account or returns outwards account and the credit total for the month posted to this intermediary account, and then a **transfer** made of the returns to the credit of purchases account when the trading account is made up. In any event, the returns will ultimately be deducted from the purchases total in trading account, so that the figure for *purchases will be shown net*.

RETURNS OUTWARDS BOOK (4) **BOUGHT LEDGER**
David Brown (52)

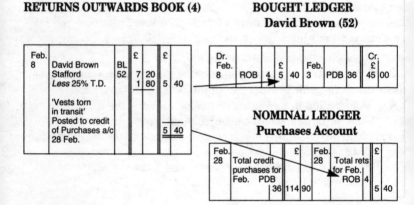

NOMINAL LEDGER
Purchases Account

A similar procedure is adopted with the sales returns. The net value of the goods returned is taken straight form the returns inwards book to the credit of the customer's personal account in the sales (debtors) ledger, thereby reducing his indebtedness. The total of the returns inwards book for the month will be taken to the debit of sales account (or an intermediary returns inwards account if one is in use), and the turnover figure on trading account will be shown *net*, i.e. total sales less returns inwards.

Where VAT is applicable, again there will be the need for additional columns in the returns books (see the next chapter).

Assignment

KEY POINTS

1 The writing up of ledger accounts is fairly simple, as long as you establish, from the outset, whether the account to be written up is in the bought ledger or the sales ledger.

Be careful where contra sales take place (as in the problem below). Put yourself in the place of the business owner and *balance up his books for him.*

2 As with credit purchases and credit sales, the cash book is not affected by the physical return of goods and crates. The book-keeping entries simply entail a reversal of the original transaction, or at least part of it.

Sometimes, though, cash sales are returned, and then the money would be refunded via the cash book.

3 In any return of goods, ask yourself immediately, 'Has trade discount been deducted from the original transaction?'

4 The treatment of returns may affect the trial balance totals. Check whether purchases and sales have been shown as *gross* or *net*, and whether returns appear under *their own heading* on the trial balance. This could account for the difference between the textbook answer and your own TB total (which may not be wrong, after all).

15.1 Write up the account of Julian Morton in the books of The Midland Agency from this information for the month of March.

March		£
1	Balance brought forward	84.40
3	Credit sales to Morton	56.20
	He paid his February account	
12	Further sales to Morton	36.30
	Allowance for returns	2.50
22	Bought some special fittings and equipment from Morton	22.60
25	Returned some damaged parts bought on 22 March.	
	Morton sent credit note to adjust	4.80
31	Balanced the account	

16

VAT AND PAYE

Introduction

Any business will have to deal with tax, but initially the only contact with the tax authorities may be for the business proprietor to pay **income tax** on the profit made. However, as a business expands there are two other taxes it is most likely to come into contact with, and where it will act as an unofficial tax collector for the Government. These are **Value Added Tax** (VAT) and **Pay As You Earn** (PAYE), the system for deducting tax and national insurance from the wages paid to employees.

At this level, no detailed knowledge of either is required, but you do need to know how to deal with the accounting entries that they may generate. It helps to understand those if you learn a little about the taxes involved.

Value Added Tax

VAT is a tax on goods and services. As its name suggests, it is intended to be a tax on the value added at each stage, until the product or service is bought by the consumer.

Example

Peter Smith buys sheet steel from John Brown for £100 and forges it into 100 spoilers for cars. He sells the 100 spoilers to Iqbal Aziz for £250. The added value is £150 (£250 – £100).

Iqbal Aziz spray paints the spoilers so that they will match the cars. He sells them to David Adams for £450. The added value is £200 (£450 – £250).

David Adams fits the spoilers to customers' cars for £10 each, plus tax. If he can sell and fit all 100 spoilers he makes £1000, and the added value is £550 (£1000 – £450).

For the sake of the example, assume that VAT is 10%. When Peter Smith buys the steel for £100, the vendor will add 10%, so he will actually pay £110. John Brown has to hand over the £10 VAT to Customs & Excise, who are responsible for administering the VAT system.

When Peter Smith sells the spoilers he will also add VAT to the **full** sale price, a tax charge of £25. When he works out what he owes Customs & Excise, he is allowed to deduct the £10 VAT he paid out from the £25 collected, and pay over the balance, £15. This, it should be noted, is the VAT at 10% on the *value he has added* of £150.

Similarly Iqbal Aziz adds £45 to the cost of the spray painted spoilers he sells to David Adams. Mr Aziz pays Customs & Excise £20 – the £45 VAT he has collected *less* the £25 he has paid out. Again this is 10% of the value he added, £200.

Finally David Adams adds £1 to the £10 cost of each of the spoilers he sells and fits. He collects £100 in VAT, deducts the £45 he paid, and hands over £55 to Customs & Excise.

In total Customs & Excise have collected 10% of the final sale price of the spoilers – £100 in all, but they have collected it from each trader in proportion to the value he added.

Trader	Value added	Tax due	
John Brown	£100	£10 – 0 =	£10
Peter Smith	£150	£25 – 10 =	£15
Iqbal Aziz	£200	£45 – 25 =	£20
David Adams	£550	£100 – 45 =	£55
Total	£1000		£100

A business does not have to register for VAT unless its taxable supplies in the previous twelve months exceed £47 000, although it may register voluntarily with a turnover below this figure. This figure, and the VAT rate and fraction given in this chapter, are as at April 1996.

A business which is not registered for VAT will enter all its costs inclusive of any VAT charged, it will not separate out the VAT. A business which is registered has to have separate analysis columns for the VAT, as will be explained below.

Dependent on the particular supply of goods or services, a supply may be **exempt** from VAT, **zero-rated**, or charged at the **standard rate** which is currently 17.5%. Although there are important differences for tax purposes between exempt and zero-rated supplies, the consequence for book-keeping is the same – no VAT is included. All other supplies which the business pays for (known as the **inputs**) will include a sum for VAT, and all supplies it makes (known as the **outputs**) will have to have VAT added to them. If the invoice for an input only gives a total cost including VAT, the amount of VAT can be found by using the current VAT fraction. At present it is $\frac{7}{47}$, so if an item costs £94 including VAT at 17.5%, the VAT is $\frac{7}{47} \times$ £94 = £14, and the price before VAT is £80.

In order to record the VAT, the day books of a VAT-registered trader will have extra columns to account for VAT. On the purchases side, there will now be three columns – **Net**, **VAT** and **Total**. The amount in the Total column for each transaction, the total of the net cost plus the VAT, is the amount which is posted to the credit side of the supplier's account.

At the end of the month or whenever the books are posted, the separate totals for net cost and VAT are debited respectively to the purchases account and to the Customs & Excise account in the nominal ledger.

Similarly on the sales side there are again three columns – Net, VAT and Total. The amount in the Total column for each transaction is posted to the debit side of the sales ledger for that customer, and in due course the totals of the net and VAT columns are credited to the sales account and to the same Customs & Excise account in the nominal ledger as was used for the purchases. A similar process is followed for returns.

Returning to the illustration of the purchases day book procedure set out in Chapter 13, the transactions are now shown with VAT included. To make the calculations simpler the VAT rate is assumed to be 10% – in an examination you will be told what rate of VAT to use.

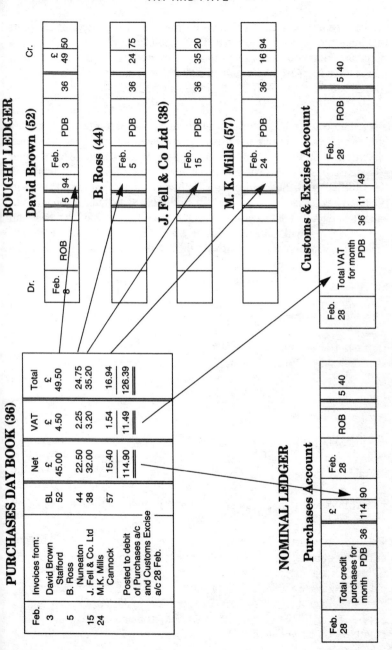

PURCHASES DAY BOOK (36)

Feb.	Invoices from:	BL	Net £	VAT £	Total £
3	David Brown Stafford	52	45.00	4.50	49.50
5	B. Ross Nuneaton	44	22.50	2.25	24.75
15	J. Fell & Co. Ltd	38	32.00	3.20	35.20
24	M.K. Mills Cannock	57	15.40	1.54	16.94
			114.90	11.49	126.39
	Posted to debit of Purchases a/c and Customs Excise a/c 28 Feb.				

BOUGHT LEDGER

David Brown (52)

Dr.					Feb.			Cr. £
Feb. 8	ROB		5	94	Feb. 3	PDB	36	49 50

B. Ross (44)

				Feb. 5	PDB	36	24 75

J. Fell & Co Ltd (38)

				Feb. 15	PDB	36	35 20

M. K. Mills (57)

				Feb. 24	PDB	36	16 94

Customs & Excise Account

Feb. 28	Total VAT for month	PDB	36	11	49	Feb. 28	ROB	5	40

NOMINAL LEDGER

Purchases Account

Feb. 28	Total credit purchases for month	PDB	36	£ 114	90	Feb. 28	ROB	5	40

— 89 —

It can be seen that the figure debited to the purchases account remains the same, £114.90, *less* the £5.40 of returns, giving a total of £109.50. However, the amounts owed to Brown, Ross, Fell Ltd and Mills have increased by a total of £10.95, so in due course they will be paid £120.45. The extra £10.95 is the £11.49 debited to the Customs & Excise account *less* the £0.54 credited on the returns.

The sales side is dealt with in a similar way – look again at Chapter 14. When the additional columns had been included as explained above, if VAT were added at 10%, £13.26 would be added *in total* to the debtors' accounts. The amount credited to sales in total would still be £132.60, and the additional £13.26 would be credited to the same Customs & Excise account. It is the *net balance* on the account that is due to Customs & Excise (or, if it is a debit balance, due from them as a repayment), which in this case is £2.31. So the Customs & Excise account at the end of the month would look like this:

Dr.	**Customs and Excise Account**					Cr.
Feb.			£	Feb.		£
28	VAT input total for			28	Returns outward book	0.54
	February PDB 36		11.49	28	VAT output total	
28	Balance due to				for February	13.26
	H.M. Customs c/d		2.31			
			13.80			13.80
Mar.				Mar.		
				1	Balance b/d	2.31

It may help to realise that, in accounting terms, this money does not 'belong' to the business. All that the business is doing is acting as an unpaid tax collector: collecting VAT on behalf of Customs & Excise on the goods or services it sells, and offsetting the VAT it has to pay on its purchases. The net balance is handed over to Customs & Excise on a periodic basis.

The normal pattern is that a business produces quarterly **VAT returns**, submitting them together with any payment on or before the end of the month following the end of the quarter. So, for example, a business on a January/April/July/October quarterly cycle would have to deliver a return for the three months to January by the end of February, for the three months to April by the end of May, and so on. It follows that the Customs & Excise account will not normally ever drop to zero, since by the time the VAT due for the three months to January is paid, transactions for February will have been entered.

Customs & Excise Account
4 months ended February

VAT input totals from PDB			VAT outputs totals from SDB		
30 Nov.	Nov. total	3 100	30 Nov.	Nov. total	4 800
31 Dec.	Dec. total	2 400	31 Dec.	Dec. total	3 000
31 Jan.	Jan. total	2 800	31 Jan.	Jan. total	3 700
31 Jan.	Bal. c/d	3 200			
		11 500			11 500
			1 Feb.	Bal. b/d	3 200
28 Feb.	Feb. total	2 200	28 Feb.	Feb. total	3 300
28 Feb.	Bank	3 200			

—— PAYE ——

Pay as you earn, or PAYE, is the system under which the income tax and national insurance contributions due from *employees* is deducted from their pay by their employer who then pays it on to the Inland Revenue. Strictly speaking national insurance contributions are payable to the Contributions Agency, but the Inland Revenue acts as collector on their behalf.

The details of how the tax and national insurance due are calculated is beyond the scope of this book, and is not covered in accounting or book-keeping examinations. You only need to be aware of the basic terms involved, and how the transactions are entered in the books.

An employee will be entitled to a certain amount of **gross pay**, which may vary with overtime, piecework, holidays etc. Say for example that for a given week an employee's gross pay is £200. Using a code number issued by the Inland Revenue and a set of tax tables, the employer will calculate the income tax due on this pay under PAYE. Say for example this comes to £30. The employer then uses another set of tables to calculate the national insurance contributions (NIC) due – this might be £15. The total of these two, £45 in our example, is often referred to as the **deductions from gross pay**, or simply as

deductions. This amount is not paid out to the employee, but is kept back by the employer and paid over on a monthly basis to the Inland Revenue. The employee actually receives £155 in our example (£200 – 45) which is called the **net pay**.

Again, in order to understand the accounting it is important to understand what is happening. The employee is actually entitled to £200 in pay. However, this employee also has to pay £30 to the Inland Revenue and £15 to the Contributions Agency. To make sure that they get their money, the PAYE system requires the employer to hold this amount back and only give the employee the net pay, with the balance being paid over to the Inland Revenue in settlement of the *employee's* tax liabilities.

Assume that there are ten employees all paid the same as the one in the above example. The total gross pay for the business is therefore £2000, and this is the amount debited to the wages account. The cash actually drawn out to make up the ten employees' wage packets will be the total net pay of £1550, so this is the amount credited in the bank account. The remaining £450 is credited to the Inland Revenue account, showing the Inland Revenue as a creditor for this amount until it is paid over at the end of the month.

There are two further complications.

- As well as the NIC that is deducted from the employee's pay, the *employer* also has to make NIC payments based on the wages paid to the employees. The accounting entries for these are simply to debit the wages account again and credit the Inland Revenue account.
- The second point to note is that it is only the tax and national insurance in respect of employees that are dealt with through the PAYE system. The income tax and national insurance paid by a sole trader or a partnership based on the trading profit is not an expense of the business at all – it should be treated as drawings. However, if the business is run as a limited company, the main shareholders may well be directors. Any salary that they are paid is subject to PAYE in the normal way.

17

CLASSIFICATION OF LEDGER ACCOUNTS

There are two main divisions of ledger accounts:

- **personal accounts** of people, firms and companies relating in the main to the credit accounts of suppliers and customers.
- **impersonal accounts**, subdivided into:

  - **real and property accounts**, comprising 'fixed assets' such as premises, machinery, motor vans, furniture and fittings, and 'current assets' of stock on hand, money at the bank and in the office
  - **nominal accounts**, relating to the firm's sales revenue and the expenditure incurred in creating that revenue. These accounts include profits and gains (sales, commissions earned, rents and discounts received) and also losses and expenses such as wages and salaries, advertising, rent and rates payable, repairs, lighting and heating, insurance, and miscellaneous expenses.

General rules for posting

	Personal accounts	Real/property accounts	Nominal accounts
Debit:	Who receives	Asset value coming in	Losses and expenses
Credit:	Who gives or pays	Asset value going out	Profits and gains

It is customary for all personal ledger accounts to be balanced at the end of the month, the *new balance being brought down* showing the exact amount owing to each creditor or due by each debtor. When, however, an account shows a single posting, it need not be balanced, as the *amount shown is the balance*.

In large firms credit customers' accounts are often so numerous that further sub-division of the sales ledger is necessary. It could be divided into three or more separate parts, alphabetically or geographically, for instance.

– Common forms of ledger accounts –

Dr. **Andrew White** (debtor's *personal* account) Cr.

June			£		June			£	
1	Balance b/f		10	50	3	Cheque	CB	10	50
15	Sales	SDB	18	20	17	Returns	SRB	2	20
					30	Balance c/d		16	00
			28	70				28	70
July									
1	Balance b/d		16	00					

John Norton (creditor's *personal* account)

June			£		June			£	
2	Cheque	CB	22	90	1	Balance b/f		22	90
6	Returns	PRB	3	60	5	Purchases	PDB	65	60
20	Balance c/d		96	20	18	Purchases	PDB	34	20
			122	70				122	70
					July				
					1	Balance b/d		96	20

Furniture & Fittings (a *real* account)

June			£						
1	Balance b/f		200	00					
8	Cheque	CB	60	00					
	(new cabinet)								

Motor vans (a *real* account)

June			£		June				£	
1	Balance b/f		600	00	10	Sale of old van	CB		550	00
20	Cheque for				30	Loss on sale				
	new van	CB	2800	00		(P&L a/c)			50	00
					30	Balance c/d			2800	00
			3400	00					3400	00
July										
1	Balance b/d		2800	00						

Rates (a *nominal* expense account)

June			£						
24	Cheque for ½ yr's								
	rates	CB	320	00					

Insurance (*nominal* expense account)

June			£						
5	Fire & General	CB	88	00					
29	Employers' Liab.	CB	54	00					

Commissions Received (*nominal* gains account)

					June			£	
					28	Cheque from			
						WB Agency	CB	40	00

The destination of these ledger accounts between the trial balance and the balance sheet is now shown:

	Trial Balance		T&P&L a/c		Balance Sheet	
	Debit	Credit	Debit	Credit	Assets	Liabs.
A. White, debtor	16.00				16.00	
J. Norton, creditor		96.20				96.20
Furniture/fittings	260.00				260.00	
Motor vans	2800.00				2800.00	
Rates account	320.00		320.00			
Insurance account	142.00		142.00			
Loss on sale	50.00		50.00			
(motor van)						
Commissions rec'd		40.00		40.00		

The loss (and expense) on the sale of the old van has been taken direct from the motor vans (ledger) account to the debit of profit and loss account. After the closure of all the nominal (expenses and gains) accounts by transfer of their balances to the debit or to the credit of the revenue accounts, the only accounts left with 'open' balances are the asset, capital and liability accounts. These open accounts are carried forward to the next trading period, and are shown on the skeleton balance sheet below.

Note that at this stage the whole of the profits and gains, losses and expenses of the business have been absorbed into the revenue accounts, ending with the net profit or loss on trading to be transferred to the proprietor's capital account.

	£	£
Assets employed		
Fixed assets		
Van account	2800.00	
Furniture/fittings	260.00	3060.00
Current assets		
Stock	—	
Trade debtors	16.00	
Bank and cash	—	—
Financed by		
Capital at 1 June		
Add net profit	———	
Less drawings		—
	———	
Current liabilities		
Trade creditors	96.20	
Expense creditors	—	—

Pause for thought

It is important to distinguish between a payment made (or a liability incurred) for a permanent fixed type of asset, and a revenue expense payment (or expense liability incurred). Later, in Chapter 21, this is explained in further detail.

Sometimes students are confused because *both assets and expenses have debit balances*. The main thing to bear in mind is that there is a credit entry, either in the cash book or on a creditor's account for *both asset and expense transactions*, but the ultimate destinations are quite different, as illustrated in this chapter.

Classify the following under the headings of real, personal and nominal:

- machinery
- bank overdraft
- capital
- new lease
- Judi Bray (customer)

- wages
- insurance (paid)
- rates in advance
- Delia Harlow (supplier)

Which of these ledger accounts would have credit balances?

Assignments

KEY POINTS

1   Do not credit money received from the sales of old assets to cash sales.

   The correct procedure is to credit the old asset account with the sum realised, ascertain the *loss on sale*, and debit this to profit and loss account.

   If there is a small profit, this would be credited to P&L A/c, and the asset account debited. Since the asset has been sold, it must be taken out of the books.

2   Again, note that in assignment 17.2 you are operating a contra account with your wholesaler.

3   A personal ledger account contains a financial summary of the business transactions with a certain person or firm during some part of the accounting period.

4   Both asset and expense accounts have debit balances or totals. Their destinations, though, are quite different. The asset is taken to the balance sheet, whereas the *expense is absorbed* in working out the net trading profit or loss.

5   It may help to think of the expense incurred as paid to a *named* expense account such as the Midland Electricity Board.

6   Where sums of money (or goods) are withdrawn by the proprietor, think of the *personal* drawings account as receiving or benefiting, with the business relinquishing cash or goods.

17.1 List the following under account headings of real, personal or nominal:

Cash sales £54; van repairs £16; rates £200; commission earned £28; insurance paid £35; garage extension £850; new desk bought £80; bought new fax machine £180; sale of old fax machine £25; cheque from V.J. Pauli £45 in payment of goods bought three months ago.

17.2 Post up the account of Howard Tarver, a wholesaler, from these details.

July
1 You owe Tarver £122.44 for goods bought in June.
3 Further purchases £60 less T.D. of 25%
5 Returns to Tarver £16 gross
Paid his June account
Bought further goods £72
less 25%
11 Sales to Tarver £25.50 less 20% T.D.
15 Tarver returned £5 gross goods
24 Further supplies from Tarver £36 less 25%. He also made an allowance of £2.60 for packing case returned
31 Balanced the account

17.3 Post up the account of Trevor Tongue in the books of Miller Bros and bring down the balance at 30 June.

June
1 Tongue owes Miller Bros £46.20 for supplies in May
3 Tongue buys further goods from Miller Bros to value of £80 less T.D. of 20%
5 He returns £10 gross to supplier, and settles May account
12 Further sales to Tongue £35.50 less usual discount
22 Cheque sent by Tongue for £50 'on account'. Allowance of £3.50 made for containers returned
25 Tongue's cheque returned by Bank to Miller Bros with remarks 'refer to drawer'
26 Tongue called on his creditor, handed in £40 in cash, tore up his cheque and promised balance early in July

17.4 What kind of ledger accounts would be found in the accounting department of a large wholesale warehouse, specialising in household groceries and covering the Midlands and West Country?

REVISION EXERCISE 2

1   David Shaw commenced business on 1 July with a capital of £3000 made up as follows.

	£		£
Cash in hand	30	Bank balance	2345
Fixtures/fittings	175	Van valued at	700

An amount of £250 was owing at 1 July to Roy Fenton for the van, recently acquired by the business.

After posting the above details to the cash book and the general ledger and the personal ledger account of Roy Fenton, you are required to record the transactions listed below for the month of July.

On completion of the postings, balance up all personal and nominal ledger accounts and take out a trial balance at 31 July.

July		£	
1	Bought some shelving	100.00	
	and a second-hand cupboard	20.00	
	Stamps	4.00	
3	Supplies bought for stock from Bryan Benson, subject to a trade discount of 20%	120.00	gross
5	Cash sales	45.30	
	Sold goods to Esther Allen (allowing her T.D. of £10)	70.00	gross
9	Cash sales	86.60	
	Paid cash into bank	80.00	

	Paid insurance (fire and theft)	12.50	
	Drew cheque for self	30.00	
12	Paid various advertising expenses	15.50	
	Bought further goods from Benson, being allowed 20%	150.00	gross
14	Returned goods to Benson	15.00	gross
	Cash sales	74.40	
	Sale at special price to Dinah Symonds	104.00	
	Made urgent delivery to Owen Moore	38.80	
18	Cash purchases	12.00	
	Drawings for self (cheque)	60.00	
	Cash sales	158.80	
	Sold goods to Judith Palmer (making special allowance of £22.50)	130.00	gross
23	Paid amount due on van to Roy Fenton	250.00	
26	Received payment of Miss Allen's account	60.00	
30	Paid wages for month in cash	240.00	
31	Paid rent for July	36.00	
	Paid all surplus cash over £30 into bank		

2 Copies of two of David Shaw's personal ledger accounts are shown below.

Bryan Benson

June			£	July			£
14	PRB	13	12.00	3	PDB	28	96.00
31	Balance c/d		204.00	12	PDB	35	120.00
			216.00				216.00
				Aug.			
				1	Balance b/d		204.00

Esther Allen

July				July			
5	SDB	24	60.00	26	Cheque	CB	60.00

(a) Which, of the two accounts shown, is that of the debtor? What was the position with regard to both accounts on 10 July and again on 13 July?

(b) Is the trade discount allowed by the creditor greater than the trade discount allowed to the debtor? What would be the discount percentage allowed to David Shaw in the accounting records of Bryan Benson?

18
FINAL ACCOUNTS
OF A SOLE TRADER

This chapter may appear to be the ultimate target for many students, and indeed, with the ability to comprehend and classify the various accounts of a small trader and assemble them in final account form, it may be said that perseverance and concentration has been worthwhile, even though we are still at the elementary stage.

A sole trader's final accounts are now depicted with rather more detail than that we have already seen, followed by explanatory notes.

Trading and Profit and Loss Account
for the year ended 30 June

Turnover		18 500
Less returning inwards		300
		18 200
Cost of sales:		
Purchases for year	8 000	
Stock 1 July	2 000	
	10 000	
Less:		
Stock 30 June	(2 500)	
Returns outwards	(200)	
	7 300	
Carriage inwards	120	
Warehouse wages & NIC	3 380	
		10 800
Gross profit		7 400
Commission received		680
		8 080
Salaries & NIC	2 800	
Rates	360	
Advertising	410	
Carriage outwards	130	
General expenses	180	
		3 880
Net profit, taken to capital a/c		4 200

Balance Sheet of A. Trader
as at 30 June

Assets employed			Figures for
Fixed assets	£	£	previous year
Premises at cost	10 000		
Machinery at cost	3 000		
Fixtures/fittings at cost	350		
Motor van at cost	2 650	16 000	
Current assets	£		
Stock 30 June	2 500		
Trade debtors	1 800		
Bank	670		
Cash	30	5 000	
Current liabilities			
Trade creditors	1 280		
Expense creditors	20	1 300	
Working capital		3 700	
Net assets		£19 700	
Financed by			
Proprietor's capital			
Balance 1 July	19 000		
Net trading profit	4 200		
	23 200		
Less drawings	3 500	19 700	
		£19 700	

The trading and profit and loss account

Purchases are shown less *returns outwards* to give the net figure of £7800. *Carriage inwards* (on purchases) increases the cost of the goods bought and in consequence is a trading account expense.

Closing stock at 30 June is deducted from the total costs of materials bought to give the *cost of merchandise used or consumed*, i.e £7420. To this figure is added warehousing wages (in preparing the goods for sale). This gives us the cost of the goods which have been sold to show the *cost of sales* figure of £10 800.

On the credit side of the trading account is the net turnover of cash and credit sales, a total of £18 200. The difference between the actual net sales (£18 200) and the cost of those sales (£10 800) is the gross trading profit of £7400.

Most of the profit and loss debits have originated from the cash book or from an expense voucher to be settled later by a cash payment. *Carriage outwards* is an expense of selling and distribution, debited on this lower account to distinguish it from *carriage inwards* (on purchases). *Both are expenses and debits.*

Salaries generally refer to payments made to the monthly paid staff, comprising office and administrative personnel, normally a more static figure than the wages paid on the production and warehousing side. The wages paid to office cleaners, however, should be charged to the profit and loss account.

The few items found on the credit of profit and loss account are usually recognised by the word 'received' and generally refer to small gains or miscellaneous receipts such as 'rents received', 'commissions received' and 'discounts received'.

It is important to remember than neither assets nor drawings appear in the revenue accounts, the only exception being the opening and closing stocks, needed to adjust the net debit for purchases to find the actual cost of the materials consumed during the trading period.

The balance sheet

The *fixed assets* have been listed and totalled first, in order of permanency, usually the case with merchanting and trading firms.

Premises would be regarded as more permanent and likely to be kept for a longer term than any of the other fixed assets.

Note that the valuation of all fixed assets is at cost, presumably their original cost. This is not likely to be their true worth, as wasting assets such as vehicles and machinery are subject to heavy wear and tear. Their reduction in value (called **depreciation**) is dealt with in Chapter 23.

The *current or circulating assets* are generally listed in the order shown. These assets change their form in the course of trading, stock sometimes being re-styled before the sale of the merchandise, sold to cash and credit customers (the unpaid accounts of the latter being recorded in the books as trade debtors). As the money comes in, further goods are bought for cash or on credit (thus creating trade creditors) and so the trading cycle goes on.

Bank and cash are called 'liquid assets' and petty cash is normally absorbed into the main cash or paid into the bank at the balance sheet date.

Working capital

A commercial enterprise conducts its daily activities and trading operations through the deployment of its working capital. These routine activities will include the buying, conversion and sale of merchandise, the collection of credit customers' accounts, the payment of regularly occurring expenses such as wages and salaries, postal expenses, advertising, telephone and electricity bills etc.

Working capital is not merely the cash available for use. It is the excess of current assets over current liabilities, as shown in the illustration on the balance sheet earlier in the chapter. In this instance the total of the current liabilities of £1300 is deducted from the total of the current assets (£5000) to give the working capital of this business as £3700.

Capital owned and capital employed

The capital owned by a sole trader is the final balance of the capital account. On this last balance sheet this would be £19 700. This is also the owner's equity and the net worth of the business according to the book values of the net assets.

There are several interpretations of *capital employed*, the two most common being:

- the total of the fixed and current assets available for the full use and purpose of the business (£21 000 in this instance)
- the same figure as above but excluding debtors who have the use and benefit of the firm's money (£19 200 on this reckoning).

—— Proprietor's capital ——

The capital account of the sole trader is *the proprietor's personal account* in the eyes of the business. Increased sales revenue, allowing for normal profit percentages, should increase this capital account, but money and goods withdrawn from the business for the proprietor's private use will reduce the owner's holding of net assets and also capital.

Care must be taken, in drafting the balance sheet, not to include ordinary trade creditors in the capital section, as the personal account of the proprietor shows the internal debt due by the business to the owner.

The capital account of A. Trader shown on his balance sheet is simply a vertical copy of his personal account kept in the private ledger, thus:

Dr.   **Capital Account**   Cr.

		£			£
June 30	Drawings for year	3 500	July 1	Balance b/f from last year	19 000
30	Balance c/d	19 700	June 30	Net trading profit from P&L a/c	4 200
		23 200			23 200
			July 1	Balance b/d	19 700

It will be seen that A. Trader has increased his capital (and the net assets) by £700 during the past trading year. This amount is the difference between the profit made and the sum total of his drawings.

—— Current liabilities ——

The current liabilities are the trade accounts (amounts owing to suppliers) at the date of the balance sheet, and also any business expenses not yet paid (amounts owing for printing, heating and lighting, or perhaps for wages and salaries accrued at the balance sheet date). An overdraft at the bank is also a current liability.

The adjustments necessary with regard to expense creditors are explained in Chapter 25.

Pause for thought

Make up a small trading and profit and loss account, inserting your own figures, to include:

sales, purchases, returns inwards and outwards, stocks at the beginning and at the end of the period, warehouse wages, carriage inwards and outwards, rents received, transport expenses, rates paid, salaries, postages, insurances, heating and lighting.

Show the cost of sales in the trading account.

Following the drafting of the revenue account on the above lines, continue with a balance sheet showing the layout similar to the illustration at the beginning of this chapter. Show the working capital and the net assets in completion of the assignment.

Assignments

KEY POINTS

1 The one main and useful equation in accounting is simple enough to remember:
$C + L = A$
where
C is the proprietory capital;
L the external liabilities of the business; and
A the sum total of the assets and property of the business.
When working out problems of capital, net worth and equity, given any two of these basic business elements, the third can easily be calculated.

2 In all these elementary exercises, the proprietor's capital account on the balance sheet should be presented clearly. In no circumstances should either trade or expenses creditors be jammed into the capital section.

18.1   Refer back to Revision Exercise 2 and make up the trading and profit and loss account for the month and a balance sheet as at 31 July from the trial balance already extracted, taking the valuation of Mr Shaw's closing stock at 31 July to be £45.

.8.2 Make up the trial balance and a complete set of accounts, as at
30 June, from the following balances extracted from the financial books of Lucian Lane, a small retail merchant whose business is mainly cash with a small credit connection.

Show clearly on his balance sheet:

(a) separate headings for fixed and current assets, the capital,
and current liabilities.
(b) In a balance sheet show Mr Lane's working capital and his
net assets at 30 June.

	£
Capital account 31 May	2000
Carriage inwards	42
Cash balance 30 June	67
Bank balance 30 June	1850
Carriage outwards	56
Warehouse expenses	235
Petrol and oil	86
Fittings and fixtures	340
General expenses	28
Returns inwards	66
Returns outwards	44
Van repairs	52
Stock 31 May	320
Purchases	3682
Sales	8760
Insurance	34
Advertising	44
Rent and rates	420
Stationery	32
Trade creditors	220
Drawings	800
Salaries	1600
Trade debtors	430
Van at book value	840

Mr Lane valued his closing stock at £480.

19

INTERPRETATION OF ACCOUNTS

The trading account determines the gross profit (or loss) over a defined period of trading, providing useful information to management, in particular when comparisons are made with the trading accounts of other periods, or with those of competitors.

To arrive at some of the bases of comparison, namely the cost of sales, gross profit percentages and the rate of stock turnover, a simple and old-fashioned horizontal style of trading account is first shown:

Trading Account
for the month of January

		£			£	£
Stock 1 Jan.		800	Cash sales		450	
Purchases	£5000		Credit sales	£5800		
Less returns	300	4700	Less returns	250	5550	6000
		5500				
Less stock 31 Jan.		1000				
Cost of sales		4500				
Gross profit		1500				
		6000				6000

Cost of sales

The cost of sales (or the cost of the goods sold) is found by simple arithmetic on the debit side of the trading account by adding the opening stock to net purchases and deducting the figure for closing stock. This cost of sales figure is not the same as the goods bought or purchases, but the valuation of closing stock probably includes much of the merchandise recently bought.

The cost of sales figure is also increased by other trading account debits such as wages, carriage inwards and warehousing expenses, omitted here for simplicity.

Gross profit and mark-up percentages

The trading results of one period may be compared with those of another period (or of a competitor) by expressing their gross profits as percentages of their relative sales turnovers. In the trading account illustrated the percentage is arrived at thus:

$$\frac{\text{Gross profit}}{\text{Net sales}} \times 100, \quad \text{that is} \quad \frac{1500}{6000} \times 100 = 25\%$$

This might be regarded as a fair gross profit percentage, but to a large extent it would depend upon the nature of the business.

If there were a wide variation between the gross profit margins of one period and the next (and it is not a seasonal business) management would investigate the reason for the discrepancy.

This percentage is different from the one which is used by the trader to arrive at a selling price, known as the **mark-up**. The mark-up percentage is the amount by which the cost of the goods *to the trader* is to be increased to arrive at the selling price, i.e. gross profit over cost of sales. In the above example it would be:

$$\frac{1500}{4500} \times 100 = 33.3\%$$

Rate of stock turnover

The number of times the stock in trade is turned over in the course of a month or a year has a direct bearing upon the gross profit of a business. Generally, profit increases if the rate of stock turnover can be improved and the cost of sales remains fairly proportionate to the turnover.

The rate of stock turnover is calculated by dividing the *cost of sales by the average stock*.

The average stock in the illustration is: $\dfrac{£800 + £1000}{2} = £900$

The rate of stock turnover is then:

$\dfrac{\text{Cost of sales}}{\text{Average stock}}$ that is $\dfrac{4500}{900} = 5$ times in the month.

Comparison of stock turnover

Study these figures for two separate businesses in the same trade. Which do you think is the more successful of the two?

	Average stock	Stockturn	Mark-up on cost
Business A	£1000	6 times a year	30%
Business B	£1000	10 times a year	20%

Business A has a much higher mark-up percentage than Business B, yet the trading results of the latter are the better of the two, as not only is the turnover of B increased on its lower profit margin, but the gross profit of B is also greater than that of A, as now shown.

Business A	Stock turnover	$£1000 \times 6$	$= £6000$
	Gross profit	$6000 \times \dfrac{30}{100}$	$= £1800$

Business B	Stock turnover	$£1000 \times 10$	$= £10\,000$
	Gross profit	$10\,000 \times \dfrac{20}{100}$	$= £2000$

— Comparison of business profits —

From the information tabled below you are asked to give your opinion, supported by percentages, as to which business (operating in the same trade) seems to be the more progressive of the two.

	Capital employed £	Turnover £	Gross profit £	Net profit £
Business A	7 500	6 000	3 000	1 500
Business B	10 000	8 000	3 600	1 800

At first glance, the second business may appear to be more progressive, until it is noticed that the greater gross and net profit of Business B are based upon its greater (by one-third) capital and turnover than Business A, leading then to the natural assumption that the gross and net profits of Business B should be even larger than those shown.

A comparison by percentages will show the issue in a better perspective.

(a) Percentage of gross profit to turnover:

Business A $\quad \dfrac{£3000}{6000} \times 100 = 50\%$

Business B $\quad \dfrac{£3600}{8000} \times 100 = 45\%$

(b) Percentage of net profit to turnover:

Business A $\quad \dfrac{£1500}{6000} \times 100 = 25\%$

Business B $\quad \dfrac{£1800}{8000} \times 100 = 22.5\%$

(c) *Percentage of gross profit to turnover:*

Business A $\qquad \dfrac{£1500}{7500} \times 100 = 20\%$

Business B $\qquad \dfrac{£1800}{10\,000} \times 100 = 18\%$

This comparison by percentages reveals that Business A, though operating on a smaller capital, is the more progressive business, provided, of course, that the figures given for both businesses are truly representative for their trade, with abnormalities excluded.

Liquidity ratios

One of the reasons for looking at the accounts of a business may be credit control – seeing whether it is appropriate to extend credit to it for goods purchased. In this case it is not so much the profitability of the business that matters but its ability to pay its debts as they fall due. This in turn means that it must have readily realisable liquid assets. Two main ratios are used for considering whether this is so.

- The **current ratio** is the more traditional of the two, comparing all current assets (generally stock, debtors and cash) over current liabilities. It is generally accepted that this ratio should be over 2 – i.e. current assets should exceed current liabilities by the ratio 2:1 at least. However the problem with this ratio is that it treats a business as liquid even if it has a high level of stock which simply cannot be sold.
- The alternative ratio, and the one often relied on more for credit decisions, is the **acid test ratio**. This is the same as the current ratio, but excluding stock. It is normally thought that this ratio should be at least 1, on the basis that it can then pay its creditors as they fall due out of the money it receives from its debtors.

Care should be taken in interpreting these ratios too strictly. An expanding company may well have ratios which look adverse but, provided it has sources of working capital (such as a bank overdraft facility still unused), it will still be liquid and worth doing business with.

Assignments

KEY POINTS

1   In problems concerning cost of sales or stockturn, always make up a modern style trading account showing the deduction of closing stock on the debit side of the trading account.

2   A critical appraisal of trading account figures might invoke these questions:

- Are the figures as good as expected?
- Are the figures as good or better than those of the previous year?
- Are certain lines more profitable than others?
- Should economies be made in some departments?
- Is money or stock being embezzled and what precautions should be taken?

19.1   The balances below were extracted from the books of Norman Deal on 31 January. Find his gross and net profit percentages on turnover; also his rate of stock turnover.

	£		£
Stock 1 Jan.	600	Net purchases	2300
Stock 31 Jan.	900	Net sales	6250
Warehouse expenses	205	Salaries	430
Carriage inwards	45	Advertising	80
Carriage outwards	50	Wages	1500
Rent and rates	400	General exes.	40
Heating/lighting	160	Comm. rec'd	535

19.2   Say which, in your opinion, is the more profitable of the two businesses, from the figures given below. Give your reasons.

	Average stock	Stock turn	Mark-up on cost
	£		
Business RS	2000	6.5 times	40%
Business KC	2000	8.5 times	32%

REVISION EXERCISE 3

Gregory Bartel's balance sheet at 30 June was made up on these lines:

Assets employed	£	£	£
Fixed assets at cost			
Premises	5000		
Fittings	300		
Motor van	1800		7100
Current assets			
Stock	900		
Trade debtors	696		
Bank	1250		
Cash	54	2900	
Less: Current liabilities			
Trade creditors	825		
Rates owing	175	1000	1900
			9000
Financed by		£	£
Proprietor's capital		6000	
Loan from Mrs G. Bartel		3000	9000
			9000

Your assignment is to open a new set of account books from the information given above, and then post up Gregory Bartel's trading transactions for the month of July, as listed below from the original entry stage.

The trade creditors comprised two suppliers' accounts, viz. Hugo Jones £550 and Mohammed Ali £275, totalling £825 on the above balance sheet.

The trade debtors' total of £696 comprised four accounts, namely:

Hilary Fane	£180	Delia Harlow	£162
Petula Hill	£144	Richard Mead	£210

Balance up all accounts and take out a trial balance on 31 July. Make up the trading and profit and loss account for Gregory Bartel for the month of July, and a balance sheet as at 31 July, accepting his own valuation of closing stock at £860.

Transactions for July:

July

1 Bought £160 of goods from Hugo Jones, being allowed 25% trade discount
   Cash sales £84
2 Paid creditors for rates £175
   Cash sales £141; paid £100 into bank
6 Drew cash from bank and paid wages £150
   Miss Fane sent cheque for £180 in settlement of her June account
   Paid £300 'on account' to Hugo Jones
   Bought £80 desk for office; paid by cheque
9 Cash sales £165; paid £100 into bank
   Paid advertising account £20, and garage account £25
12 Daily takings amounted to £137
   Paid £150 wages out of cash
   Repaid Mrs Bartel £500, reducing loan account to £2500
14 Received cheque for £162 from Delia Harlow. She bought another £60 of goods. Allowed her 20% trade rate.
15 Cash sales £159; cash purchases £18
18 Paid wages £160
   Sold £80 of merchandise to Petula Hill less 10% trade rate:
   She paid £100 off her outstanding account.
23 Bought £240 of goods from Hugo Jones, being allowed the usual discount. Also paid £15 delivery charges in cash.
   Bought £120 of goods from Mohammed Ali who would only allow £10 trade rate. Gave him a cheque for £275 in settlement of his June account.
25 Returned £40 (gross) merchandise bought from Hugo Jones on 23 July
   Cash sales £136; paid £160 wages out of cash
28 Sold £75 of goods to Dinah Mortimer allowing her 20% trade discount.
   Paid £6 carriage on various deliveries made during the month of July.
30 Cash sales £128
   Withdrew £100 cash for private and family use
31 Paid £80 cheque to a part-time typist working from her home address.
   Retained £25 cash for office and paid surplus cash into bank.

20

CASH FLOW STATEMENTS

Introduction

In a very simple trading situation, the movement of cash is exactly the same as the profit or loss. Say a market trader buys flowers for her Saturday market stall costing £300 and sells them for £600 (throwing away any she cannot sell, as they will not last until the next week's market). She also pays £40 on the day for the hire of the market stall. Her profit is obviously £260, and the amount of cash in her pocket has also increased by £260.

However, it only takes a slightly more complex business for the cash and profit and loss account position to diverge. If the florist in the example above was in a market that opened every day, then stock could probably be kept for a day or two. If she had £50 of stock at the end of the day, her cash would still have increased by only £260 but her profit would have increased by £310, as the cost of sales would be £300 of purchases less £50 of stock.

While the balance sheet and profit and loss account will normally give a better picture of how a business is doing, it is undoubtedly true that control of cash is an important issue in a business, and seeing what has happened to cash during the year can sometimes throw light on the accounts. Larger organisations are therefore generally required to produce cash flow statements as part of their financial statements.

Cash flow

Purpose of a cash flow statement

The *starting point* for a cash flow statement is the reported net profit or loss. The *finishing point* is the total increase or decrease in cash and bank balances. Both of these figures are of course easily identifiable in the balance sheet. The purpose of the cash flow statement is to reconcile the one to the other. This is normally done in three sections:

cash flows from operating activities
cash flows from investing activities
cash flows from financing activities. These are considered in turn shortly.

In making these adjustments, it is important to remember which way the adjustment needs to go. The statement starts with profits and ends with cash. Anything that increases profits but does not increase cash must therefore be *subtracted*, anything which reduces profits but does not reduce cash must be *added*. Similarly, anything that increases cash but does not increase profits must be *added*, anything which reduces cash but does not reduce profits must be *subtracted*.

Cash flows from operating activities

As the title suggests, this is the section where trading adjustments are detailed. The main examples of this are:

Changes in stock Increases in stock will increase profits (by reducing cost of sales) but will not increase cash, so if stock has gone up the increase must be deducted in the computation, if it has reduced it must be added.

Changes in debtors An increase in debtors means profits increased but no increase in cash, so if debtors have gone up the difference must be subtracted, if debtors have gone down it must be added back.

Changes in creditors This is the reverse of debtors, so if creditors have gone up the difference must be added back, if they have gone down the difference must be subtracted.

These adjustments will be required in virtually all cases. The following three adjustments may not be quite so all-pervasive, but will be found in a majority of statements.

- **Depreciation** Because this is a book entry that reduces profits it has to be added back in the statement.
- **Loss/profit on sale of fixed assets** Because this is essentially an adjustment for insufficient or excess depreciation, a loss is added back and a profit is deducted. The actual proceeds from the sales are dealt with under investing activities.
- **Other provisions** Where provisions have been made for possible expenditure not yet incurred, they must be cancelled out in the cash flow statement. The most common example is a bad debts provision, against debts that are still in the debtors' total but where payment is unlikely. So if, as is normal, a provision has resulted in a net expense in the profit and loss account, it must be added back in the cash-flow statement. Rather less likely, a provision made in a previous year may have been reduced, resulting in a net addition to profits. This must be subtracted.

Cash flows from investing activities

Essentially these are transactions affecting the fixed assets part of the balance sheet. Whilst the profit or loss on a sale of fixed assets has now been adjusted for, the fact that *what was a fixed asset is now cash* has not. This increases cash without increasing profit and must therefore be added. The main adjustments are:

- **Sale of equipment etc**. As detailed in the previous paragraph, the cash received for such a sale must be added in the statement.
- **Purchase of equipment etc**. Correspondingly, a purchase of equipment will have reduced the cash balance of the organisation without having had a direct effect on profit. This must be deducted in the statement.
- **Investments** The principles for investments are similar; a purchase of shares in another company (for example) is a reduction in cash and must be subtracted in the statement, whereas a sale of an investment increases cash without increasing profits, and must be added. Adjustments for investments must be distinguished from financing, covered below. Investments are investments made in other organisations, financing are the investments made by others in the reporting organisation.

ash flows from financing

ιe most immediate form of bank financing, the overdraft, will show
automatically in the cash flow statement when it finishes with
sh and bank balances. However, all other financing movements
ed to be accounted for, including the return on financing received
those who provide it.

Drawings This is the return that a proprietor of an unincorporated
business receives. Since it is a reduction of the cash in the business
that does not affect profit, it has to be deducted.

Capital introduced If capital is brought into the business,
whether from the proprietor or a third party, the cash balance will
increase without any corresponding increase in profit, so this has
to be added back.

Capital repaid Most often this will be the repayment of a loan,
but in partnerships it can be the repayment of partnership capital.
As the opposite of capital introduced, it has to be subtracted in the
calculation.

Dividends and interest on loans Similar in concept to drawings,
dividends and interest on loans represent the return that investors
expect on their capital invested in the business. As such they
reduce cash without affecting profit, and must therefore be
subtracted in the calculation.

Preparation of a cash flow statement

ow that the adjustments to be made are understood, it is possible to
ok at the preparation of a cash flow statement. Given a balance sheet
nd profit and loss account, with comparative figures, the statement
hould be straightforward to prepare, and has an inbuilt check since
ιe calculation should end with the change in bank and cash balances
s shown.

Example

ook ahead to Chapter 25, and you will find a balance sheet and profit
nd loss account for Robert Morris. Before preparing the cash flow

statement, you need some more information about the previous year's balance sheet, which would be in the column headed 'last year's figures'. The figures you need are these (some of them are referred to in the profit and loss account):

Stock	£1200
Debtors:	£2000
less a provision of £120	(£120)
Cash at bank (not overdrawn):	£2065
Rates in advance:	£350
Cash in hand:	£55
Trade creditors:	£1000
Expense creditors:	£750

The only change to fixed assets from the previous year to the current year is that machinery and equipment were purchased during the current year for £3000. The advertising expenditure carried forward was also £200 last year.

The cash flow statement is as follows.

Cash flow statement for Robert Morris			
Cash flow from operating activities:	£	£	£
Net profit		2890	
Increase in stock	(250)		
Depreciation	760		
Decrease in debtors	200		
Reduction in bad debt provision	(30)		
Increase in prepayment	(50)		
Increase in trade creditors	400		
		1030	
Cash flow from investing activities:			
Purchase of equipment		(3000)	
Cash flow from financing:			
Drawings		(3745)	
Decrease in cash			(2825)
Bank balance at end	(730)		
Cash balance at end	25		
		(705)	
Bank balance at start	2065		
Cash balance at start	55		
		2120	
Decrease in bank/cash balances			(2825)

21
CAPITAL AND REVENUE EXPENDITURE

The term **capital** so far has been used to indicate the net worth or equity of various small businesses, and in particular the personal capital accounts of sole traders.

Sometimes, though, the term is used to describe *capital assets* acquired for the permanent use of the business, and the expenditure used to purchase or extend those assets is then known as **capital expenditure**, and would include land and buildings, plant and machinery, furniture and fixtures, motor vehicles and office equipment.

On the other hand, **revenue expenditure** refers to the cost and expense of maintaining and operating these capital assets, including all renewals and repairs; in addition, revenue expense embraces all costs of maintaining sales revenue and relates to all normal trading and business activities involving the payment of wages and salaries, materials bought for re-sale or conversion, advertising, insurance, electric power, heating and lighting, repairs, renewals and transport of all description, in fact all those debits and charges to be found on the trading and profit and loss account.

Capital expenditure

A new business starting from scratch might have only a sum of money in the bank as its sole asset. In the course of trading, various fixed and permanent assets would be acquired, probably some fixtures and fittings, some machinery and perhaps a motor van. The payment for these capital assets would be made either from the original money capital, or from profit surpluses retained by the business. This is capital expenditure.

Again, these (or similar) assets could be acquired in the purchase price when a business is bought as a 'going concern', and any further payments made on improving or extending these assets would be debited to these same accounts and increase their 'book value' as now illustrated.

Dr. **Machinery Account** Cr.

			£				
Jan.1	Balance b/f		4500				
May 5	Cheque (new machine)	CB	1200				

Furniture and Fixtures

			£				
Jan.1	Balance b/f		720				
Oct. 15	Cheque (filing cabinet)	CB	40				

Vans Account

			£				
Jan 1.	Balance b/f (second-hand van taken over)		1800				

At the end of the financial year, the balances of these asset accounts would be shown on the balance sheet under the heading of *fixed assets*, thus:

Assets Employed

Fixed assets	£	£
Machinery at cost	5700	
Fittings at cost	760	
Vans at cost	1800	8260

Revenue expenditure

Revenue expense is charged and written off to the trading account or the profit and loss account at the end of the financial year, as now shown.

Dr.				**Warehouse Expenses**			Cr.
			£				£
Mar. 4	Cheque for re-decorating, etc.	CB	420.00	Dec. 31	Transfer to trading account		498.00
May 12	Cleaning	CB	24.00				
Aug. 6	Cleaning	CB	24.00				
Nov. 22	Cleaning	CB	30.00				

Advertising

			£				£
Jan. 6	Cheque	CB	15.50	Dec. 31	Transfer to P&L a/c		68.70
Apl. 3	Cheque	CB	28.20				
Oct. 15	Cheque	CB	25.00				

Van Repairs and Renewals

			£				£
Mar. 25	Red Garage (service & new exhaust	CB	68.50	Dec. 31	Transfer to P&L a/c		120.90
Sept. 2	Service, etc.	CB	52.40				

Trading and Profit and Loss Account
for period ended 31 December

	£		
Warehouse expenses	498.00		
Gross profit b/d	—		
	===		===
Advertising	68.70	Gross profit c/d	—
Van repairs/renewals	120.90		

Money received from the sale of capital assets is debited to the cash book and *credited to the related asset account*. Receipts of this nature are not regarded as revenue income like sales and cash takings. Remember that an old asset has been sold and its book value must now be erased from the accounting records. This means that the balance remaining on the account (normally a small debit balance) must be written off to the profit and loss account, as it is a loss and expense suffered by the business. In more advanced accounting there is an adjustment in connection with its depreciated book value if the asset has been subject to a depreciation charge.

The distinction between capital and revenue expenditure is important, as the charging of heavy capital outlay against profits reduces (often substantially) the net profit and the tax liability of the business.

Revenue Expense	Capital Expense
is debited and charged to the profit and loss account, thereby decreasing the net trading profit with the consequent reduction of the income tax assessment.	is debited to the asset account and taken to the balance sheet under the heading of *fixed assets*. Capital expenditure must not be charged against profits.

Assignments

> ## KEY POINTS
>
> 1 The term 'revenue' refers to *either income or expense* having a direct connection or influence on the trading returns or profits of the business.
>
>   Revenue expense is charged and debited against profits, whereas revenue income implies additional profit or gain.
>
> 2 Money spent on repair work and renewals (including redecoration) is *revenue expense* and is debited to profit and loss account.
>
>   Money spent on improvements or extensions to existing capital assets is *capital expenditure* and must be debited to the asset account.

3 In examination problems on capital and revenue expenditure, ask yourself: Has the money been used up in the ordinary course of trading (rent, stationery, wages, etc.), or will its use and benefit extend perhaps over a number of years (as in the case of a new van, office equipment or a building extension)?

Another point about a building extension or the erection of machinery is that the *wages paid to the firm's own workers engaged on the erection work is also capital expenditure* to be debited to the cost of the asset.

21 Re-draft this trading and profit and loss account of Miranda Moss, incorrectly drawn up by her younger brother.

Trading and Profit and Loss Account
as at 31 August

	£		£
Stock 31 July	680	Sales	7200
Purchases	3440	Rets. inwards	60
Rets. outwards	26		
Carriage outwards	18	Stock 1 July	550
Wages	520		
Salaries	1240		
Gross profit c/d	1886		
	7810		7810
Stationery	15	Gross profit b/d	1886
Drawings	360	Loss on sale of van	130
Van repairs	45	Sundry receipts	68
Rents received	84	Carriage inwards	42
Second-hand van	830	Net loss on trading	54
Sundry expenses	26		
Advertising	24		
Answering machine	96		
Showroom extension	580		
Decorating office	120		
	2180		2180

20.2 A firm bought some new machinery for £5000 on 1 January The first year normal running costs were £150, and wages of £350 were paid to an engineer for his time spent on checking and improving its output. Discuss charges to capital/revenue at the year-end.

Pause for thought

Allocate the following debits between capital and revenue:

- repairs to van
- rates and taxes
- fire insurance
- purchase of five-year old computer
- set of new tyres for van
- purchase of a second-hand filing cabinet
- petrol and oil account
- donation to charity.

In what circumstances would a motor vehicle be regarded as a current asset?

22

THE GENERAL JOURNAL

We have already used journals (day books) in connection with the original entries for credit purchases and credit sales. Another subsidiary book, the **general journal**, is now brought into use as a memorandum record for transactions of a special or unusual nature which cannot conveniently be taken to another book of original entry.

In the UK, the general journal does not form part of the double entry system, but is used as an aid or a guide to help the ledger clerks with their postings. Sometimes examination questions will ask for an answer in journal form, even though it would not actually be dealt with in this way by a book-keeper. The advantage of asking for the answer in this form is that it provides a structured and succinct way to check whether the student understands the question.

Opening entries

In some examination problems the proprietary capital at the start of the exercise is not disclosed. The student may be expected to find the commencing capital of the owner/proprietor from a list of assets and liabilities such as the following:

Fittings £250;   Machinery £1700;   Opening stock £1400;
Trade debtors: Jones £245   and   Brown £105
Trade creditors: Evans £65   and   Smith £210

In addition to the assets and liabilities listed above, Frank Lawson, new owner of this business, after settlement of all commitments with vendor, has the sum of £575 in the business bank account.

The first stage in this type of problem is to list the opening assets and liabilities in the journal in trial balance style, thus:

Opening Entries   1 July

		Debit £	Credit £
Fittings		250	
Machinery		1700	
Stock on hand		1400	
Bank		575	
Debtors: Jones		245	
Brown		105	
Creditors: Evans			65
Smith			210
Capital F. Lawson			4000
		4275	4275

the difference or balancing figure

The commencing capital of Frank Lawson is worked out by addition the subtraction to give the balancing figure of £4000, also confirmed by the simple accounting equation of $A = C + L$, where A represents the assets, C the proprietor's capital, and L the external liabilities of the business.

If this problem formed part of an exercise, the asset balances would be posted to the debit of their respective accounts in the cash book, the sales ledger and the general ledger; the balances owing to the two creditors would be posted to the credit of their accounts in the bought ledger. In this manner Frank Lawson's new set of accounting books would be put on a proper double entry basis as from the beginning of the trading period commencing 1 July.

It is not usual to total journal entries except in the case of opening entries as shown in the illustration. From the examples below, it will be seen that these details are merely recorded in the journal so that the ledger clerks will understand the reason for the entries and be able to post the debits and credits to their correct locations.

Note the orthodox method of journalising by recording the debit entry first in the left-hand column, with the credit entry underneath in the right-hand column, the wording slightly indented to the right of its upper counterpart.

The brief explanation of the journal entry, typed or written before ruling off the entry, is called the **narration**.

The General Journal

			£	£
	Special entries			
March 5	Cash	Dr.	25	
	Fittings/Fixtures a/c			25
	Being sale of old cupboard			
June 30	Bad debts account	Dr.	14	
	Alan Jones			14
	Irrecoverable balance written off to Bad Debts a/c			
	Correction of errors			
July 9	T.N. Johnson	Dr.	8	
	T.H. Johnstone			8
	Payment from T.H. Johnstone had been incorrectly posted to the credit of T.N. Johnson			
Sept. 2	Machinery Repairs a/c	Dr.	15	
	Machinery (asset) a/c			15
	Adjustment of item wrongly charged to asset account			
	Year-end transfers			
Dec. 31	Trading Account	Dr.	9100	
	Stock at 1 Jan.			270
	Purchases for year			8640
	Carriage inwards			190
	Transfer of year-end balances			

———— Trial balance errors ————

The agreement of the trial balance totals should confirm the arithmetical accuracy of the books, but there may be certain undisclosed errors only brought to light through a good system of internal check, a rigid method of control, and in some instances simply the passage of time or a subsequent audit of the books. Five kinds of these errors are now listed.

- **Error of omission** This occurs when goods are bought or sold on credit, but the original documents in connection with the purchase or the sale are forgotten or mislaid. In consequence, neither the debit nor the credit entries are posted in the books.
- **Error of duplication** In this instance the original records become duplicated and the customer is charged double the amount that is actually owing. Normally, this is found and rectified fairly quickly once the monthly statement of the supplying firm has been sent out.
- **Error of commission** This occurs when the amount, usually a payment, is debited or credited to the account of the wrong person. On the previous page, a payment of £8 was received from T.H. Johnstone but was incorrectly credited to the account of T.N. Johnson, and has now been adjusted through the journal.
- **Compensating error** Mistakes in arithmetic of similar amounts, often round figures of £10 or £100 commonly occur in additions, subtractions or carry-forwards, in particular in the day book and when the accounting system is not computerised. For example, the bought day book may have been over-cast by £100 in a carry-forward, and an error also made of £100 on one of the big debtors' accounts with the balance at £100 less than it should be. This would be corrected through the journal by a debit of £100 to the debtor's account and a credit of £100 to purchases account.
- **Error of principle** An amount may have been posted to an expense account instead of to an asset account, or vice versa. Again, see previous page, where the machinery repairs account is being debited, through the journal, with £15 which in the first instance has been wrongly charged to the asset account. This is an important aspect of capital and revenue expenditure.

Pause for thought

Describe the function of the general journal and the purpose in this country for which it is used, more as an aid to the book-keeper/cashier than as an integral part of the double entry system. In what way does the general journal differ from the bought and sales journals?

Of the five kinds of trial balance errors which might, for a while, remain undetected, say in which category you would place the following:

- A £100 error in the carry-forward of the bought journal, offset by £100 error in the addition of the cash sales total

- Wages of £400 paid to own workers in erecting their new welding machine, the expense payment being debited to trading account
- George Green has been invoiced £15 for goods ordered and sent to Miss Georgina Green.

Assignments

KEY POINTS

1 The necessary requisites of a journal entry are:

- The date is entered in the journal.
- The account to be debited is first shown, with the amount in the first column.
- The account to be credited is shown underneath, indented slightly to the right, with the amount in the second (credit) column.
- A brief explanation of the purpose of the entry, called the narration, is given before ruling off. With the exception of opening entries, totals are not necessary.

2 In examination problems, where errors are to be corrected through the journal, you are told that *something is wrong*, that a *mistake has been made*, and you are asked to put it right.

All that is necessary is to *reverse the whole or part* of the incorrect posting already made. As long as you can comprehend what is wrong, it will be simple enough to put it right.

3 Some answers only need a single-sided correction. For example, the sales day book has been over-added by £100 to show an excess of £100 on the sales account. Instead of altering the ledger account, a single-sided journal entry is made on the debit of the journal. This is picked up by the sales ledger clerk and posted to the debit of sales account, to give the correct balance on this account.

22.1 Write up the opening journal entries of Wensley Dale's business from the information given below, and ascertain his commencing capital at 1 January.

	£		£
Premises	6000	Mortgage loan of	5000
Fittings	550	(secured on premises)	
Stock	1010	Machinery at cost	2500
Bank	865	Van valued at	1750
Cash	35	Rates owing	290

Trade debtors:		Trade creditors:
Leo Fraser £425	:	£320 Lesley Mansel
Abe Fisher £160	:	£185 Petra Nutkins

22.2 Journalise the following.

March

2 Bought second-hand word processor and paid by cheque £175

5 Cash purchases £138

12 £52 of goods sold to Anthony Fircone

15 Bought £130 of goods from Horace Heap

20 Sold old typewriter for £45 cash

22 Paid £5 for stationery

27 Drew £50 cheque for 'self'

31 Transferred opening stock of £950 to trading account at month end

22.3 Make the necessary corrections, through the general journal, of the following.

July

1 A new fax machine bought for £250 has been debited to purchases account.

3 Sales of £38 on credit to Sue Palliser have been wrongly charged to her sister Sarah.

6 A cheque for £20 from A. J. Smith has been credited to the account of his cousin J. A. Smith.

12 Drawings of £25 were found debited to salaries account.

15 Repairs to machinery £75 have been debited to machinery (asset) account.

18 The purchase of a filing cabinet (£80) has been charged to stationery account.

28 The total of the purchases day book for June was found to have been posted to purchases account as £986 instead of the true figure of £968.

30 Bank interest received at end June £8.50 was debited to bank charges account.

REVISION EXERCISE 4

Perdita Gale has a small trading business. Her assets and liabilities are listed at 1 March:

	£		£
Warehouse premises at cost	8000	Stock at 1 March	920
Fittings/fixtures at cost	350	Bank balance	475
Loan from bank (secured on premises)	4000	Cash in hand	55

At this date her trade debtors comprised three accounts:

Maud Foster £48   Judi Birch £60   Melanie West £42

Money was owing on three suppliers' accounts, namely:

Giles Stevens £80   Keith Owen £30   Rupert Kent £140

You are required to open a new set of books and post up Miss Gale's assets and liabilities, including her opening capital. Then you are to post up all the listed transactions shown opposite for the month of March, make up her trading and profit and loss account for the month, and draw up a vertical style balance sheet as at 31 March.

Miss Gale valued her closing stock at 31 March at £850.

The balance sheet of Miss Gale should show clearly her working capital and net assets. Also calculate her gross profit percentage on turnover and the net profit return in her commencing capital at 1 March.

March

2   Cash sales £78
    Sold goods £35 to Judi Birch less 20% trade discount.
    She paid her February account less 5% cash discount.

4   Cash sales £86; paid £50 into bank.
    Miss Birch returned £5 gross purchases of March 2.

6   Paid part-time assistant wages £50 in cash and applied to
    Inland Revenue for her PAYE tax code number, and also made
    contact with Ministry of Social Security with regard to weekly
    contributions.
    Paid stationery £4 and stamps £2 in cash.

9   Bought £60 of goods from Rupert Kent less 25% T.D. Paid £5
    carriage on purchases. Settled Kent's February account less 5%
    cash.

11 Returned £12 (gross) merchandise to Rupert Kent.
    Bought £85 filing cabinet; paid by cheque.

14 Sold £72 of goods to Maud Foster. She paid her old account. Also
    sold £38 of goods to Melody Robson and opened up new credit
    account.

15 Cash sales £126. Cash purchases £6. Paid delivery charges on
    routine credit sales £3 cash. Paid wages £50.

19 Bought £80 of merchandise from Giles Stevens and settled his
    February account less 5% for cash. (*Note*: 'for cash' often implies
    'by cheque'.)

22 Received credit note for £12 from Giles Stevens for trade discount
    on the purchases of 19 March.

25 Cash sales £140. Paid £50 wages.
    Miss Gale withdrew £100 cash for private use.

30 Paid local secretarial agency £60 for temp.

31 All surplus cash above £20 paid into bank.

23
DEPRECIATION OF FIXED ASSETS

Machinery and vehicles lose value through wear and tear and the passage of time, and in business the loss in value is regarded as an expense in the same way as any other routine expense of the business. Money has been paid out which will never be recovered, and to assess the true or approximately true trading profit of the business this loss in value of a fixed asset, which is called **depreciation**, must be taken into account. It is a common but mistaken assumption that the depreciated value of an asset should approximate its second-hand value. The purpose of depreciation is to allocate the total capital outlay over the useful life of the asset, so that the reported profits accurately reflect the true costs of earning them.

Most fixed assets (the big exceptions being land and buildings) are subject to permanent shrinkage in value due to wear and tear (vehicles), the passage of time (leases), obsolescence (changes in method, style or fashion), or simply through general wastage and being used up or worked out in the case of coal and lead mines.

– Elementary depreciation methods –

In elementary book-keeping, it is customary to show the value of each fixed asset on the balance sheet at its commencing book balance as at the beginning of the financial year *less* the deduction for depreciation as charged against profits, the final amount and up-to-date value of the asset in the balance sheet corresponding with the adjusted ledger balance of the asset.

The accounting entries are thus.

- a *debit* to profit and loss account of the depreciation amount, reducing the trading profit, and
- a *credit* to the particular asset ledger account, with the consequent reduction of its book value.

Apart from the annual and periodic re-valuation of a fixed asset (like loose tools) with the difference in value being adjusted against profits, the two main depreciation methods encountered at first-year level are known as the **fixed instalment method** and the **reducing instalment method**, best explained by illustration.

Ten-year Lease – fixed instalments of £1000 a year

			£				£
Year 1 Jan. 1	Cheque (original cost)		10 000	Dec. 31 Dec. 31	Depreciation P&L a/c Balance c/d		1000 9000
Year 2 Jan. 1	Balance b/d		9 000	Dec. 31 Dec. 31	Deprec. P&L a/c Balance c/d		1000 8000
Year 3 Jan. 1	Balance b/d		8 000				

Van Account – 25% on the reducing balance

			£				£
Year 1 Jan. 1	Cheque (original cost)		3200	Dec. 31 Dec. 31	Deprec. P&L a/c Balance c/d		800 2400
Year 2 Jan. 1	Balance b/d		2400	Dec. 31 Dec. 31	Deprec. P&L a/c Balance c/d		600 1800
Year 3 Jan. 1	Balance b/d		1800				

Note the difference between the two methods of elementary depreciation illustrated. The ten-year lease is depreciated by equal instalments of £1000 a year, whereas the van is depreciated by 25% on the *reducing balance of the account*, the depreciation instalments charged against profits also reducing each year.

The sections of the profit and loss accounts and the balance sheets applicable to the depreciation charges and the fixed asset account details will be shown thus:

Profit and Loss Account

Year 1			£	£				
	Deprec. of lease		1000					
	Deprec. of van		800	1800				
Year 2								
	Deprec. of lease		1000					
	Deprec. of van		600	1600				

Balance Sheet

Year 1	Fixed assets	£	£	£
	Lease	10 000		
	Less depreciation	1 000	9 000	
	Van			
	Less depreciation	800	2 400	11 400
Year 2	Fixed assets			
	Lease	9 000		
	Less depreciation	1 000	8 000	
	Van	2 400		
	Less depreciation	600	1 800	9 800

Scrap value

In instances where fixed instalment of depreciation is adopted for machinery or vehicles, the working life of the asset is first estimated, and its likely scrap value on sale or disposal. The scrap value is then deducted from the original cost of the asset, and the residual amount divided by its estimated number of working years, to give the annual charge against profits for *fixed instalment* depreciation.

Say a machine's original cost is £4000, and its working life estimated at 12 years, with a possible scrap value of £400 on its replacement. The fixed annual charge for depreciation would be (£4000 – £400)/12 = £300 a year.

– Provision for depreciation account –

Aspects of depreciation with a view to replacement costs in today's inflationary world vary a good deal and belong to more advanced accounting. A legal requirement of the Companies Acts, however, in so far as limited companies are concerned, is that fixed assets must be shown on the balance sheet at their cost price, the revenue account being debited in the normal way with the annual charge for depreciation with the corresponding credit being taken to a Provision for Depreciation Account, instead of taking it to the credit of the asset account.

This method is more informative to all those interested in the true finances and net worth of a company. The aggregate and cumulative depreciation is built up in the Provision for Depreciation Account, and deducted in total each year, from the original cost of the asset, shown on the balance sheet, in this way:

Machinery Account
(Depreciation by fixed instalments
of £500 a year via provision account)

Year 1 Jan.1	Cheque for new machine	CB	£ 5000				

Provision for Depreciation Account

Year 1 Dec. 31	Balance c/d		£ 500	Year 1 Dec. 31	Profit & loss a/c		£ 500
Year 2 Dec. 31	Balance c/d		1000	Year 2 Jan. 1 Dec. 31	Balance b/d Profit & loss a/c		500 500
				Year 3 Jan. 1	Balance b/d		1000

The profit and loss account will be debited with the fixed amount of £500 a year, and the asset will be shown on the balance sheet at its *original cost less aggregate depreciation*, thus:

Year 1	Fixed assets Machinery at cost Less aggregate deprec.		£ 5000 500	£ 4500
Year 2	Fixed assets Machinery at cost Less aggregate deprec.		5000 1000	4000

Depreciation fund and investment account

The adoption of the provision for depreciation account is simply a change in the book entries and balance sheet presentation. It does not provide for the replacement of the asset at the end of its working life. This further aspect of accounting, where an investment account is opened to provide a replacement fund for the purchase of a new machine (or perhaps a new lease) is beyond the scope of this elementary textbook, and reference to it must be brief, similarly with the next paragraph on the Statements of Standard Accounting Practice.

Accounting standards

In more advanced accounting, accounting standards lay down fundamental concepts and rules of procedure. Accounting standards are explained in Chapter 36, but one of the earliest insists that revenue accounts and balance sheets will not show 'a true and fair view' of the presentation of the figures unless certain key concepts are followed.

These key concepts would naturally be explained to students on the more advanced courses, and certainly where the final accounts of limited companies are involved. Briefly, these accounting concepts are known as:

- the **prudence concept**, concerning the actual revenue profit received (not anticipated in advance)
- The **going-concern concept**, where the belief is that normal trading will continue as before
- the **accruals concept**, which lays down that all revenue earned and expense incurred, whether paid or not, shall be brought to account
- the **consistency concept**, where the same or similar methods of treatment or valuation are applied each year, and any variation is disclosed.

Pause for thought

Explain what a wasting asset is: give one or two examples, and say how the depreciation should be dealt with in the accounting records.

- What is the purpose of writing off depreciation? Is the value of the asset increased by these entries in the accounting records?
- Apart from normal wear and tear, give two further instances where merchandise could lose value over a period of time.
- Why does the depreciation account provide a more accurate picture of an asset's value on the balance sheet?
- In addition to dealing with the paper entries involving depreciation, what safeguard should be taken to ensure that a certain machine can be replaced at the end of its working life?

Assignments

KEY POINTS

1 The loss in value of fixed assets is a business expense and chargeable against revenue. If not accounted for, the balance sheet does not present a true picture of the net worth of the assets.

2 The writing off of depreciation as a business expense does not in any way affect the cash position of the business. It is purely a book entry or paper adjustment at this stage. In advanced stages of accounting old and obsolete assets are often replaced at the end of their useful life, and various investment safeguards and funds are explained to students.

3 When a fixed asset such as a machine or a vehicle is sold, the sum realised on sale is debited to cash and *credited to the asset account*.

The depreciation charges that have been written off in the past are calculated to the date of the sale, and a profit or loss figure ascertained, as the asset must now be *eliminated from the books* .

The balance or difference left on the asset account is finally transferred to profit and loss account.

23.1 A machine is anticipated to have a working life of 15 years with a scrap value of one-tenth of its original cost at the end of that period. The original cost was £3000. What kind of depreciation charge should be written off each year if the fixed instalments method is adopted?

23.2 A lease costs £8000 for the term of ten years. Show the asset account for the first two years under what you might consider an appropriate depreciation method.

Special machinery costing £4000 is bought on 1 January. Show the machinery account for the first two years, calculating depreciation on the fixed basis of 15% on the reducing balance of the asset.

23.3 Rory Macadam asks you to prepare, from this abbreviated form of trial balance, his final accounts as at 31 December, taking note of the adjustments for depreciation shown underneath.

	£	£
Capital a/c 1 Jan.		8 000
Gross profit on trading		9 300
Drawings for year	4 500	
Debtors/creditors	1 250	880
Carriage on sales	45	
Sundry expenses	85	
Machinery 1 Jan.	5 400	
Additions during year	600	
Van account 1 Jan.	1 200	
Fittings/equip. 1 Jan.	520	
Discounts	50	60
Wages owing 31 Dec.		300
Salaries for year	4 200	
Stock 31 Dec.	2 200	
Bank overdraft 31 Dec.		1 510
	20 050	20 050

Allow for depreciation as follows:
(a)   10% on the original cost of the machinery which was £9000 (Ignore additions, as these were bought in December.)
(b)   20% on the ledger balance of the van account
(c)   5% in fittings/equipment account.

24
BAD DEBTS AND PROVISION FOR BAD DEBTS

The balances of those debtors who cannot or who persistently refuse to pay their accounts, may, after a period of correspondence, be eventually 'written off' to a **bad debts account**, although proceedings for the recovery of the money owing may continue for some time. Debts which are regarded as irrecoverable, like other business losses and expenses, are transferred at the end of the trading period, via the bad debts account, to the debit of the profit and loss account.

Later, should the debt or part of it be recovered, the sum received will be debited to the cash book and credited to a **bad debts recovered** account. Alternatively, the amount recovered from an old debtor may simply be taken to the credit of the current bad debts account, thereby reducing the *net* debit for the year.

Note, however, that amounts recovered from past defaulters are *not credited to their old personal accounts* in the sales ledger as these accounts will have been closed.

Provision for bad debts

Some debts are doubtful, not necessarily bad, though in time a proportion may prove to be irrecoverable. A *specific provision* for bad debts, covering those debts regarded as doubtful, is sometimes made on the lines now to be described. Note that this *provision is additional* to any debts known to be bad that are being written off as deemed irrecoverable.

The provision is normally a small percentage (perhaps 2 or 3%) of the total debtors' balances (net balances after deducting actual bad debts already written off).

In the first instance, when creating the new provision, say 3% of net debtors of £2000, profit and loss account would be debited with £60, and a credit for the same amount (£60) taken to a new account headed **provision for bad debts account**. The credit balance on this account is shown as a deduction from the trade debtors' total under current assets in the balance sheet. It is important to bear in mind, though that *this is a paper entry, simply a provision against a possible contingency only*, as all traders and businesses would like to see their doubtful accounts recovered in full.

Once created, the provision account remains a credit balance in the books, subject to annual adjustment, usually dependent upon the increases or decreases in the trade debtors' total at the end of the financial year. In the illustration now shown, note that after the first year (the creation of the provision) only the amount of the *provision increase is debited to revenue*; alternatively, any *provision decrease is credited back to revenue*.

	Debtors' listed totals at year-end £	Actual bad debts to be written off £	Bad debt provision
Year 1	2100	100	3% of net balances
Year 2	3150	150	3% of net balances
Year 3	2565	65	3% of net balances

The actual bad debts (in the centre section) will be transferred from the sales ledger accounts to the debit of the bad debts account, and then written off to the profit and loss account at the end of the trading year.

Dr.   **Provision for Bad Debts Account**   Cr.

		£			£
Year 1	Balance c/d	60	Year 1	P&L a/c (3% of £2000)	60
Year 2	Increased prov. carried down at end of second year c/d	90	Year 2	Balance b/d	60
				P&L a/c (provision increase to 3% of £3000)	30
Year 3	Decreased prov. to 3% of £2500 P&L a/c	15	Year 3	Balance b/d	90
	Balance c/d	75			
			Year 4	Balance b/d	75

Profit and Loss Account

		£			
Year 1	Bad Debts a/c	100			
	Prov. for B/Ds a/c	60			
Year 2	Bad Debts a/c	150			
	Prov. for B/Ds a/c	30			
Year 3	Bad Debts a/c	65	Year 3	Prov. decrease written back	15

Balance Sheet

		£	£
Year 1	Current assets		
	Trade debtors	2000	
	Less provision	60	1940
Year 2	Current assets		
	Trade debtors	3000	
	Less provision	90	2910
Year 3	Current assets		
	Trade debtors	2500	
	Less provision	75	2425

Note that the actual bad debts each year are first deducted from the sales ledger balances *before* the operation of the provision. When first created, the new provision amount (£60) is debited to the profit and loss account and credited to the new provision account. The trading profit is reduced by this £60, and on the balance sheet the trade debtors are reduced by the same amount.

In the second year, the net debtors' total has increased to £3000. Again, maintaining the same provision percentage, the provision is now to be increased to £90 (3% of £3000). But there is already a credit of £60 on the provision account, so that it is only necessary to debit an additional sum of £30 to profit and loss account in this second year. The corresponding credit is taken to the provision account, thereby increasing the provision to £90 at the end of this second year.

In the third year, the total of the trade debtors has been reduced to £2500, so that a provision of £75 (3% of £2500) only is required for this year. But since we already have a credit of £90 on the provision account, £15 of this credit balance will now be recouped by the reverse process of crediting the profit and loss account with the £15 written back, and debiting the provision account with £15. This now leaves the balance of £75 as the adjusted and correct new provision as at the end of the third year.

Note that it is always the final adjusted figure on the provision account which is to be deducted from the trade debtors' total shown under current assets on the balance sheet.

Pause for thought

- What is the difference between writing off as a bad debt the account of a defaulting customer, and the creation of a specific provision for bad debts?
- Explain the difference between insolvency, being financially embarrassed temporarily, and being made a bankrupt.

Assignments

KEY POINTS

1 Sometimes the provision account is combined with the bad debts account, the balance of the joint account being taken to the profit and loss account at the year end.

2 The main difference between the two accounts, though, is that the bad debts account is a record of actual loss and expense suffered by the firm, whereas the provision account

---

may be looked upon as more of a form of insurance against possible loss, and to show the trade debtors on the balance sheet at a conservative figure.

3 Amounts recovered from past defaulters are credited to the current bad debts account, or sometimes to a bad debts recovered account. In either case, they serve to reduce the actual bad debts at the end of the trading session.

4 After the creation of a new provision for bad debts, only the *difference between the old and the new provisions* is transferred to the profit and loss account, to the debit if an increase and to the credit if the provision is reduced.

5 The net total of the trade debtors (with actual bad debts already deducted) is shown under current assets on the balance sheet, *less the last credit balance* shown on the recently made up provision for bad debts account.

24.1 Luellen Blake has built up a small but profitable retail business, mainly on credit trade. Three years ago her accountant introduced an annual provision of 5% as a safeguard against bad and doubtful debts.

Her trade debtors' balances for last year totalled £4300 and for the current year £5800. The actual bad debts written off debtors' accounts and transferred to the bad debts account amounted to £32 this year, and a payment of £24 had been received on account of an old debt written off two years ago.

Make up Miss Blake's bad debts and her provision for bad debts account for the year just ended at 31 December.

24.2 On 30 June a year ago, the provision for bad debts in Matthew Cole's books showed a credit balance of £440. During the year he had written off actual bad debts of £72, and an amount of £18 was recovered from an old customer who had returned from Melbourne; his ledger account had been written off two years ago. Trade debtors' balances for the current year totalled £7400.

You are required to maintain the provision at 5%, make up the main accounts affected, and show how the profit and loss account of Mr Cole is adjusted.

24.3 On 31 December, the following sales ledger balances were extracted from the books of Cavendish Smith.

	£		£
Angela Ward	280	Godfrey Bean	63
Trisha Benton	98	Rebecca Lawson	158
Pamela Potter	86	Oliver Fairfax	165

During the trading year ended 31 December two small accounts totally £36 had been written off to bad debts account. The trustee in bankruptcy of one of these debtors on 20 December paid a dividend of 25% on Cavendish Smith's claim for £24.

The bad debt provision on the previous balance sheet was £48. It was decided to reduce this to 4% on the total debtors' balances for this year.

Make up the bad debts and provision for bad debts account, and show how the provision account will appear on this year's balance sheet.

25
YEAR-END ADJUSTMENTS

The costs and expenses *incurred* during an accounting period are not necessarily those which are paid during that same period. The *real income*, too, earned during that period, may also be quite different from the actual payments received from customers and income from other sources.

Certain adjustments and amendments with regard to the trading profit of a business have been explained in the last two chapters. Further adjustments are often necessary to arrive at the true expenditure and the correct trading profit.

Prepayments or payments in advance

A payment made in advance indicates that money has been paid before the last date of the accounting period for a *benefit still to be received* (in the next accounting period). This often applies to local rates, where advance payment is always demanded, and to various insurances paid on certain dates throughout the business year, normally providing cover for the full calendar year.

The adjustment is made on the nominal account, the amount not yet used up being credited to the account and brought down as a debit balance, and shown on the balance sheet under the heading of *current assets*. The revenue debit is reduced by this advance payment, thus increasing the trading profit by the same amount.

In the example now shown, the annual premiums are paid to the insurance company on 31 March and 30 June providing cover for the full twelve months. Assuming the financial year ends on 31 December, a proportionate adjustment must be made charging only £21 against the profits in this year, and £11 is carried forward for unexpired insurance, and shown as a current asset on the balance sheet.

Dr.				**Insurance Account**			Cr.
			£	Dec.			£
Mar. 31	Cheque	CB	20	31	P&L a/c		
June					¾ of £20 = 15		
30	Cheque	CB	12		½ of £12 = 6		21
				31	— Prepayment c/d		11
			32				32
Jan. 1	Balance b/d		11				

– Accrued or outstanding expenses –

Certain expenses may be owing at the date of the balance sheet. Among these typical expenses are wages and salaries due to the firm's own employees, and accounts probably invoiced but unpaid for advertising, gas, electricity and printing.

Again, a two-way adjustment is involved, this time *increasing the debit to revenue*, and bringing down, on the actual expense account, the *amount owing as a credit balance*, to be shown under current liabilities on the balance sheet.

Weekly wages when paid in cash are normally paid on a Thursday or a Friday, made up to the preceding day or sometimes two days beforehand.

In the wages account shown below, the sum of £9040 has actually been paid out up to 28 June, but since the firm's financial year ends on 30 June, two days' pay (say £80) is owing to the daily paid employees at the balance sheet date.

The wages account is adjusted in this way:

Dr.			Wages Account		Cr.
		£			£
June 30	Total wages actually paid (CB summary)	9040	June 30	Trading account (Wages paid plus) wages due)	9120
30	Wages owing c/d	80			
		9120			9120
			July 1	Creditors for wages b/d	80

The credit balance on wages account will be shown on the balance sheet at 30 June, following trade creditors, under current liabilities.

Adjustments in final accounts: Illustration

Robert Morris owns a small machine shop and retail business. The following balances were extracted from his books on 31 December, the end of his financial year.

Trial Balance   31 December

	£	£
Capital account: R. Morris 1 Jan.		30 000
Drawings for year	3 500	
Freehold premises at cost	25 000	
Machinery/equipment a/c bal. 1 Jan.	3 000	
Fittings, book balance 1 Jan.	400	
Van, book balance 1 Jan.	600	
Trade debtors/creditors	1 800	1 400
Bank overdraft		730
Cash in hand	25	
Bad debts provision account		120
Purchases and sales	8 500	23 250
Returns inwards/outwards	110	75
Carriage on purchases	145	
Carriage on sales	185	
Lighting/heating	330	
General expenses	665	
Discounts allowed/received	95	270
Commissions received		2 135
Advertising	400	
Bad debts written off	25	
Wages (storehouse and shop)	8 000	
Office salaries	4 000	
Stock on 1 January	1 200	
	57 980	57 980

In making up the final accounts of Robert Morris as at 31 December, the following adjustments and amendments are to be taken into account.

(*a*) Stock at 31 December valued at £1450.

(*b*) Rates pre-paid £400 (in general expenses account).

(*c*) Wages owing on 31 December £600; salaries owing £150.

(*d*) The bad debts provision account stands at £120 in the books. The provision for the current year is to be reduded to 5% of the debtors' total at 31 December.

(*e*) During the year Mrs Morris, wife of the proprietor, had taken goods for family use amounting to £245 at cost.

(*f*) fittings are to be depreciated by 10% of their book value; vans by 20%, and machinery and equipment also by 20% of their book value at 1 January.

(*g*) Carry forward 50% of the advertising debit, as this was recently incurred, and the benefit expected in the New Year.

(*h*) The lighting/heating debit for £330 is to be split evenly between the trading account and the profit and loss account.

The model answer to this exercise should prove useful to the student for reference. The trading and profit and loss account is left in the old-style horizontal format, so that the debits and credits can be followed more easily.

Trading and Profit and Loss Account
for the year ended 31 December

	£	£		£	£
Stock 1 Jan.		1 200	Sales	23 250	
Purchases	8 500		*Less* returns inwards	110	23 140
Add carriage inwards	145		Stock 31 Dec.		1 450
	8 645		NB Closing stock is		
			credited to trading account		
Less returns outwards £75			simply to emphasise a few of		
& goods for own use 245	320	8 325	the additional debits		
			in this instance.		
Wages	£8 000				
Wages owing	600	8 600			
Lighting/heating (50%)		165			
Gross profit c/d		6 300			
		24 590			24 590
Salaries	£4 000		Gross profit b/d		6 300
Add salaries owing	150	4 150	Discounts received		270
Carriage outwards		185	Commissions received		2 135
Lighting/heating (50%)		165	Decrease in bad debt		
Discounts allowed		95	provision (£120 less new		
Bad debts written off		25	provision of £90)		30
Advertising	£400				
Less carry forward	200	200			
General expenses	£665				
Less rates in advance	400	265			
Depreciation:					
Machinery/equipt.	£600				
Van	120				
Fittings	40	760			
Net trading profit					
transferred to Capital a/c		2 890			
		8 735			8 735

In many small retail businesses, some of the available stock for sale (in particular foodstuffs) is taken for the use and consumption of the proprietor's family. The correct adjustment is to *debit the owner's drawings account and credit the purchases account* at the cost price of the merchandise. In this instance the cost of the goods withdrawn by Mrs Morris (£245) is deducted from purchases on the debit of trading account, and added to her husband's drawings in the capital account section of the balance sheet.

An ordinary bank overdraft is a current liability, but a long-term loan made to the business (or a mortgage) is shown as a *fixed liability* under its own heading, positioned between the capital account and the current liabilities.

The new provision for bad debts is £90 (5% of the debtors' listed total). This new provision supersedes the old provision of £120 shown on the trial balance. This means that the £30 excess is no longer required and may now be **written back** (credited) to the profit and loss account. Remember, too, that it is always the *last provision* to be deducted from trade debtors on the balance sheet.

The reason for the carry-forward of £200 advertising has been explained in the list of adjustments. The nominal account for advertising will have been adjusted to show this £200 as a *debit balance*, but remember that the expense has already been paid, and consequently this item is a *fictitious asset as it is not realisable*. Do not confuse with rates in advance, a benefit still to be used up, and if premises became unoccupied a claim for repayment could be made.

The working capital of this business is found simply by deducting current liabilities from current assets (ignoring the advertising expenditure carried forward) thus:

	£
Current or circulating assets	3585
Less current liabilities	2880
To give the working capital of	705

Balance sheet

The balance sheet of Robert Morris as at 31 December, drawn up in the modern vertical form below, shows the net assets and the working capital of the business: comparison with last year's figures would be shown in brief in the right margin. Bear in mind, though, that a limited company balance sheet would show more detail of the *aggregate depreciation* of the fixed assets, and the capital section would be entirely different, showing the various classes of shares, reserves and undistributed revenue profits etc.

Balance Sheet of Robert Morris
as at 31 December

Assets employed				Last year's figures
		£	£	£
Fixed assets				
Freehold premises at cost		25 000		
Fittings less depreciation		360		
Machinery/equipment less depreciation		2 400		
Motor van, less depreciation		480	28 240	
Current assets	£			
Stock 31 Dec.		1 450		
Trade debtors	£1 800			
Less provision	90	1 710		
Rates in advance		400		
Cash in hand		25	3 585	
Current liabilities				
Trade creditors		1 400		
Bank overdraft		730		
Expense creditors		750	2 880	
Working capital			705	
Net assets			28 945	
Advertising expenditure carried forward			200	
			29 145	
Financed by				
Proprietary capital		£		
Capital account: Robert Morris 1 Jan.		30 000		
Add net trading profit for year		2 890		
		32 890		
Less drawings (£3500 + £245)		3 745		
			29 145	

Assignments

> ## *KEY POINTS*
>
> 1 A prepayment (or payment in advance) refers to a benefit still to be used up. The amount paid in advance is deducted from its related debit on the profit and loss account, thereby increasing the trading profit.

The debit balance brought down on the expense account is listed on the balance sheet after trade debtors.

2 Year-end adjustments are dealt with between the trial balance and final account stage. You will find it useful to mark the items affected by these adjustments with the pencilled amount of the adjustment to be made.

3 An accrual or outstanding expense (wages/salaries owing and various expense bills unpaid) increases the debit to the trading or profit and loss account and reduces the net profit. The credit balance brought down on the nominal expense account will be shown after trade creditors on the balance sheet.

In so far as *expense* creditors are concerned, think of the debt or money owing as being owed to a firm or organisation which has already supplied your own firm with gas, water, electricity etc.

25.1 This is the insurance account of a small trader at 31 December the end of his trading year.

Dr. **Insurance Account** Cr.

			£			
Mar. 31	Fire insurance	CB	36			
Jul. 1	Motor insurance	CB	84			
Oct. 31	Employers' liability	CB	18			

All payments relate to full premiums paid. Complete this account to show the correct debit to revenue at the year end, and also show the balance sheet details.

25.2 Geoffrey Webb works a five-day week. Wages owing to his employees on 30 June amounted to £662. His wages sheets made up to the last pay day in the current year totalled £18 444. Show the net debit to revenue and how the item 'Wages owing' will appear on the balance sheet.

25.3 Valerie Seal balances her books on 31 December. Among other items on her trial balance are these two debits:

Electricity £180 : Rates paid £260

The invoice for last quarter's electricity £38 was received early in the New Year. The amount of £180 refers to payments for the three previous quarters.

A cheque for £130 for the second instalment of the full year's rates had been paid on 8 October.

Miss Seal has been in business for one year. Complete her nominal ledger accounts to show the net debits to revenue, and also show how the adjusted items will appear on her balance sheet at 31 December.

EXAMINATION EXERCISE

KEY POINTS

1 In book-keeping examinations, accuracy and neatness are mark-earning features, and the ability to *work at speed* is equally important, as marks cannot be awarded for questions not attempted.

2 Establish your confidence by tackling the smaller and easier questions first, ensuring that they have in fact been answered to the best of your ability, and that you will not be penalised through running out of time in the rush work of the last half-hour.

3 Accept the fact that few examinees manage to get *their accounts* to balance. A good deal of time is lost by candidates looking for mistakes made in balancing, time which could be put to better purpose. It is likely to be far more rewarding to aim at good average marks on the examination paper as a whole, rather than spend too much time on a large question, even though this question will carry maximum marks. Work as fast as you can on the larger problems, but when difficulties occur in balancing, and after a rapid re-check there is still a difference, *proceed to the next question* with all speed. If there is still time left before the papers are handed in, you can renew your re-checking after the completion of the remainder of the paper.

1 When checking and preparing information for the final accounts of Keith Warren for his financial year ended 31 December, you make a note of the following listed items.

   (*a*) Repairs to van £68 had been charged to Van (asset) account.

   (*b*) A payment of £25 from Marilyn Ross, sub-tenant of Keith Warren, has been debited to the business rates account.

   (*c*) The trustee in bankruptcy of Sara Booth has recently sent a cheque for £36, being the first and final dividend of 40p in the pound of a sum written off her account two years ago. The firm's cashier has posted the payment to the credit of the debtor's old account.

   (*d*) Included in purchases is an amount of £820, and in wages an amount of £350, both payments made in connection with the construction of a new showroom for the business.

   (*e*) The sales ledger account of Hilton Mills has been credited with a cheque payment of £40 received from Milton Hills.

Make the necessary amendment or correction through the journal.

2 The warehouse stock of Sharon Lane was destroyed by fire in the early hours of 1 July, except for a small salvaged amount valued at £240. Miss Lane's accounting period was the normal calendar year. Her accountant provides you with this information.

	£
Stock valuation 31 December (six months previous)	2 200
Purchases (1 January to 30 June)	6 366
Net sales (1 January to 30 June)	14 880
Warehouse wages for six months	5 600

Prepare a draft trading account from this information, taking as the approximate figure for the gross profit of three-yearly average of 30% based upon the turnover of Miss Lane's business for the six months ended 30 June. State the amount of the claim for the destroyed stock to be made against the insurance company.

3 Titian Molloy owns a small dress-making business. The account balances listed below were extracted from her books at 30 June, the close of her financial accounting year.

For information only, the loan to Miss Molloy's friend Dinah Marsden is only of a temporary nature, to be repaid early in July. Interest has been waived.

Trial Balance   30 June

	£	£
Capital account 1July		12 000
Drawings for year	4 800	
Fittings/fixtures 1 July	1 420	
Additions during year	280	
Machinery/equipment 1 July	2 800	
Stock 1 July	1 450	
Purchases and returns	6 600	240
Sales and returns	280	18 680
Carriage inwards	88	
Carriage outwards	135	
Trade debtors/creditors	2 400	1 310
Expense creditors		75
Bad debts provision		160
Bad debts to be written off	120	
Wages of machinists	5 340	
Office salaries	3 800	
Discounts allowed/received	66	235
Commissions received		2 540
Advertising	1 350	
Lighting, heating and power	1 250	
Rent and rates	900	
Postages/stationery	36	
General expenses	72	
Cash at bank	1 023	
Cash in hand	30	
Loan to Dinah Marsden	1 000	
	35 240	35 240

In making up the final accounts for Miss Molloy, you are to take into account the following year-end adjustments.

(a) Closing stock at 30 June was valued at £2850.

(b) Insurance pre-paid £25 (debited to general expenses).

(c) Lighting, heating and power expense is to be apportioned between the trading account and the profit and loss account three-fifths and two-fifths.

(d) The advertising debit comprises a special campaign launched in May, and £500 is to be carried forward into the next financial year.

(e) The bad debt provision is to be maintained at 5% of the total trade debtors' figure.

(f) When questioned about goods withdrawn, Miss Molloy confirmed that she had taken material for her own use at the cost price of £180.

(g) Fixtures and fittings are to be depreciated by 20% on the book balance of the asset, including the additions.

(*h*) Machinery and equipment is to be depreciated by 20% on the book value at the beginning of the year.

4 (*a*) There is a credit balance of £120.56 in the bank column of your cash book. This has been brought down from the debit on 31 December. Would you show this on your balance sheet as a (i) fixed asset (ii) current asset (iii) current liability?

(*b*) If your bad debt provision is decreased, would this mean (i) a smaller gross profit (ii) a larger net profit (iii) an increase in trade debtors on the balance sheet?

5 Post up the office equipment account of Anita d'Alvis from the information now given.

		£
1 January	Balance of account brought forward from last year	280
22 March	New filing cabinet bought	95
17 April	Old cabinet sold for	22
	(originally cost £35; shown in books at cost)	
28 July	Bought new table and chairs	240
	Also timber for shelving	56
	Paid carpenter for work done	24
12 August	Sold old table and chairs	20
	(at original cost of £48 in books)	
5 December	Paid for repairs to an old cupboard and desk	38

6 These are entries in the rent account of RHJ Textiles Ltd:

		£			£
Jan. 5	Cheque – quarter's rent on 15 Main Street	200	Jan. 6	Cheque – quarter's rent on 20 Main Street	200

Two young sisters, Sara and Simone, came to Preston from Avignon ten years ago and took up employment at the local textile mill. They rented a house in Main Street and one sister still lives there. Sara married a wealthy widower five years back, bought another house in Main Street, and when her husband died went to live in Blackpool. The Company now pays the rent on Sara's house for one of the managers. At what address does Simone live, number 15 or 20?

26
INCOMPLETE RECORDS AND SINGLE ENTRY

Single entry

The term **single entry** implies the absence of a complete system of double entry. Whilst accountants prefer to see double entry books, single entry is the only way to deal with incomplete records. Where records are incomplete, the accountant must make use of all the available information he can find, estimating some of his figures by simple reasoning processes. The trading profit is found in this way by approximation.

Generally a rough form of cash book has been kept, and bank accounts are now in common use, even by small businesses. Year-end accounts must be made up for submission to the Inland Revenue, otherwise the trader will probably receive a grossly inflated assessment on assumed profits.

Where few records are kept

If accounts have not been prepared before, and there are neither records of business property nor of revenue income or expenditure, the visible existing assets should be verified, listed and valued. Then, checking backwards through a process of questioning and elimination, it should be possible to arrive at an approximate figure of the asset/liability position one year back.

To a large extent, the accountant has to rely upon the client's memory.

Often the biggest complication is to agree with the proprietor the amount of personal drawings. Even if a rough cash book has been kept, rarely will the physical cash on hand, or in the till, agree with the 'book' balance according to the cash book. The large discrepancy is assumed to be 'drawings'.

—————————— # Profit statement ——————————

The calculation of the profit or loss by the increased (or decreased) net worth method simply entails the listing and comparison of the known or approximated value of the assets and liabilities between the two periods, say of one year ago and today. The accounting equation $A = C + L$ is then brought into use, where A = assets, C = capital and L = liabilities.

Calculation   £

(*a*) List the known assets and liabilities at the year-end to establish the *closing capital* of 4800

(*b*) Similarly, as far as possible, list the known and approximated assets and liabilities of one year ago to establish the *commencing capital* of 3500

(*c*) *Add back* the approximated figure for proprietor's drawings 2200

(*d*) *Deduct* any additional capital brought into the business 800

Statement of Profit

	£
Increase of net assets (£4800 – 3500)	1300
Add back drawings	2200
	3500
Deduct additional capital brought in	800
Trading profit	£2700

The closing capital account, shown in its conventional form on the balance sheet, is a check on the arithmetic of this estimated profit.

Capital account	£	£
Balance 1 January (one year ago)	3500	
Additions during year	800	
Ascertained trading profit	2700	
	7000	
Less drawings for year	2200	4800

The existence of a bank account makes working on incomplete records much easier. A double entry basis can be built up from a break-down summary of the recorded items on the bank statements, together with up to date information of the fixed assets, stock valuation and lists of trade debtors and creditors.

Examination question

A typical examination question is now illustrated. A statement of affairs (balance sheet) of Adam Smith has been established as at the beginning of the trading period, one year ago. This is followed by a cash summary in total form, and there are a number of year-end adjustments to be taken into account when making up the final accounts for the year.

Cash and bank have been lumped together, quite usual in this style of question.

Statement of Affairs
as at 1 January

	£		£
Capital account: Adam Smith		Premises at cost	4000
Balance 1 Jan.	6000	Fittings/equipment	850
Trade creditors	775	Stock	930
Expense creditors	25	Trade debtors	770
		Cash/bank	250
	6800		6800

Cash summary for the year

	£		£
Cash/bank balances b/f	250	Office salaries & NIC	1 800
		Wages & NIC	2 460
Cash sales total for year	6 980	Cash purchases	326
		New counter	440
Cash/cheques from credit		Payments to suppliers	4 350
customers	5 150	Proprietor's drawings	1 800
		Insurance	95
		Rates	120
		General expenses	89
		Balance c/d	900
	12 380		12 380
Balance b/d	900		

Adam Smith's current assets and liabilities at the year-end were:
  stock £1130 : trade debtors £810 : trade creditors £660
The year-end adjustments to be taken into account are:

(a) Wages due to sales assistants £42
(b) Rates pre-paid at 31 December £30
(c) Included in general expenses is a payment of £25 for an electricity
     bill shown as owing on the statement of affairs a year ago.
(d) Another bill for £32 is now due for electricity.
(e) Depreciate fittings and equipment by 10% on closing balance.

Solution
First of all, the figures for credit purchases and credit sales are established on these lines by making up *total accounts* for both debtors and
creditors.

Total Debtors

		£			£
Jan. 1	Balance b/f	770	Dec. 31	CB receipts	5150
Dec. 31	CREDIT SALES	5190	Dec. 31	Balance c/d	810
		5960			5960
Jan. 1	Balance b/d	810			

Total Creditors

		£			£
Dec. 31	CB payments	4350	Jan. 1	Balances b/f	775
Dec. 31	Balances c/d	660	Dec. 31	CREDIT PURCHASES	4235
		5010			5010
			Jan. 1	Balance b/d	660

Note that there are four basic elements to this type of problem: commencing balances, purchases or sales for the period, payments made, and the closing balances. Given any three of these elements, the fourth can quickly be found.

Trading and Profit and Loss Account
for the year ended 31 December

	£	£	£
Credit sales			5 190
Cash sales			6 980
Total sales			12 170
Cost of sales			
Credit purchases		4 235	
Cash purchases		326	
Wages	2 460		
Wages owing	42	2 502	
Stock 1 Jan.	930		
Stock 31 Dec.	1 130	(200)	
			(6 863)
Gross profit			5 307
Salaries		1 800	
Insurance		95	
Rates	120		
In advance	30	90	
General suspenses		96	
(£89 + 32 − 25)			
Depreciation of fittings		129	
			2 210
Net profit			3 097

Balance Sheet of Adam Smith
as at 31 December

		£	
Fixed assets			
Premises at cost		4000	
Fittings/equipt.	£850		
additions	440		
	1290		
less deprec.	129	1161	
		5161	
Current assets			
Stock 31 Dec.	£1130		
Debtors	810		
Rates in advance	30		
Cash/bank	900	2870	
		8031	
Capital and liabilities		£	
Capital balance 1 Jan.	£6000		
add net trading profit	3097		
	9097		
less drawings	1800	7297	
Current liabilities			
Trade creditors	£660		
Creditors for wages	42		
Expense creditors	32	734	
		8031	

Remember that all year-end adjustments are two-sided. Both debit and credit entries are involved. Revenue gains and losses are adjusted on the profit and loss account.

——— Claims for loss of stock ———

Sometimes insurance claims for loss or damage to stock (perhaps through fire or flood) have to be based upon past records and whatever figures are available. The following is a typical elementary examination problem.

Peter West's warehouse stock was destroyed by fire on 30 June, except for a salvaged amount valued at £350. The date of the fire was exactly half way through his accounting period, and these figures were extracted from his account books and papers, kept in a fire-proof safe:

	£
Stock at 1 Jan.	1 500
Purchases (Jan.–June)	6 300
Wages for six months	3 200
Sales (Jan.–June)	12 400

A trading account was prepared from this information and a figure approximated for gross profit based upon 25% of Mr West's turnover for the current year, as this percentage had been fairly constant in recent years and was confirmed to be the average within the same trade.

Make up the insurance claim for Mr West.

Answer

Trading Account
for period 1 January to 30 June

	£		£
Stock 1 Jan.	1 500	Sales (Jan.–June)	12 400
Purchases	6 300	Estimated stock	
Wages	3 200	at date of fire	
		(£14 100 – £12 400)	1 700
	11 000		
Gross profit			
(25% of £12 400)	3 100		
	14 100		14 100

The insurance claim would be:

Estimated stock at 30 June	£1700
Less value of stock salvaged	350
	£1350

Pause for thought

There is a similarity between some 'incomplete record' type of questions and the accounts of non-trading concerns (see the following chapter). In both instances it is often necessary to establish the final cash/bank balance for the balance sheet; often, too, forms of total accounts are needed to work out the purchases/sales in one case, and the correct subscriptions for the season in the other case.

In first-level Accounting examinations, the likelihood of getting one of these problems is fairly high.

Assignments

26.1 Zoë Chapati's accountant lists her assets and liabilities at the beginning and at the end of her second trading year as follows.

		1 January £	31 December £
Stock		850	920
Trade debtors		440	550
Trade creditors		310	380
Expense creditors		—	25
Fittings and fixtures		660	1375
Loan from sister		1000	800
Bank balance		230	150

Zoë had withdrawn a regular £30 a week for her personal use, and had taken provisions from the business for family use averaging £6 a week. She had sold her private car for £600 and bought £500 of new fittings and equipment for the business out of the car proceeds. Towards the end of the year, she withdrew £1000 from the business to put down as a deposit for a new private car.

Calculate Miss Chapati's profit for the year and show her balance sheet as at 31 December.

26.2 Saffron St Cloud is a milliner. She has a high class business in the centre of Hereford. Her statement of affairs at 31 December is now shown.

		£		£	£
Capital 31 Dec.		6000	*Fixed assets*		
Current liabilities			Machinery	4400	
Trade creditors	£635		Van	600	5000
Bank overdraft	290				
Wages owing	75	1000	*Current assets*		
			Stock	1025	
			Debtors	960	
			Cash	15	2000
		7000			7000

Her transactions for the following month of January are summarised in total form and listed below:

		£
1	Cash sales (cost price of goods £175)	280
2	Paid into bank	100

3	Cash purchases	2(
4	Paid cheque for second-hand van	80(
5	Received cheque for old van	55(
6	Additional stock bought on credit	42(
7	Sales to credit customers (cost price £640)	88(
8	Sent cheques to suppliers	33(
9	Cheques received from trade debtors	59(
10	Paid expense creditors (wages owing – see BS)	7!
11	Paid various expenses in cash	3!
12	Proprietor's withdrawals in cash	4(

You are required to draft a new balance sheet for Miss St Cloud as at 31 January, taking into account all the above transactions and finding her net trading profit for the month of January.

26.3 Ralph Edwards' statement of affairs, drawn up on 1 January, a year ago, is shown in brief detail.

	£		£
Capital (the balancing figure)	16 500	Premises at cost	10 000
Trade creditors	1 500	Fittings/equipment	2 100
		Stock 1 Jan.	3 300
		Trade debtors	2 400
		Bank/cash	200
	18 000		18 000

His accountant estimated his drawings for the year at £8300, after making a cash summary of totals extracted from a rough cash book and the bank statements of Mr Edwards.

	£		£
Balance b/f	200	Cash purchases	1 800
Cash takings	18 130	Wages and NIC	6 600
Payments from		New counter & shelving	4 400
credit customers	9 270	Rates and insurance	450
		Payments to suppliers	5 500
		General expenses	120
		Drawings	8 300
		Balance in hand	430
	27 600		27 600

On 31 December, the end of his financial year, the current assets and liabilities were:

Stock £4500   Debtors £3200   Creditors £1800

You are required to make up a revenue account and a balance sheet at 31 December for Mr Edwards, taking three adjustments into the accounts:

Rates in advance £80   Wages owing £140
Fittings and equipment to be revalued at £6000.

27

NON-TRADING CONCERNS AND CLUB ACCOUNTS

Most clubs, societies and associations are **non-trading** organisations. They derive their main source of income from subscriptions and donations, and, as a general rule, allocate their surplus funds to the purpose or the project for which they have been formed; alternatively their surplus revenue is used to improve or develop their activities and amenities for their members.

— Receipts and payments account —

Small clubs and societies have few assets other than a local bank account and probably some printed stationery. The book-keeping records of this kind of organisation (where expenditure on furniture and/or games equipment is unnecessary) are simple and uncomplicated. The form of account produced by the treasurer at the end of the year or the season is easily understood by members. It is necessary only to draw up a receipts and payments account, which is simply a cash summary for the period covered by the account. There is an illustration of a receipts and payments account on the next page

The receipts and payments account, shown below, is a brief summary of money received and money paid out during the year. Every receipt, subscription and donation is included in total summary, and every payment made is also included in total form. No distinction is made between capital and revenue expenditure; this of course would probably be unnecessary in the case of a small society as all incoming cash and payments would be regarded for revenue purposes only, with no attempt made to show financial gain or loss beyond the difference in the commencing and closing cash balances.

The Over-Sixty Social Club
Receipts and Payments Account for year ended 30 June

	£		£
Cash in hand 1 July	24.50	Postages/stationery	12.20
Subscriptions rec'd		Hire of local hall	150.00
(124 members at £2)	248.00	Lighting/heating	55.40
Donations	15.00	Refreshments bought	102.80
Gross proceeds from		Prizes purchased	250.00
whist drives and		Donations to Oxfam	25.00
socials	350.00	General expenses	16.70
		Balance of cash	
		in hand 30 June c/d	25.40
	637.50		637.50
Cash in hand 30 June	25.40		

This statement is simply a summarised copy of the club's cash book, and cash and bank have simply been combined for the sake of ease in comprehension by members.

– Income and expenditure account –

The receipts and payments account is incomplete in so far as real financial information is concerned. Clubs and societies of any size acquire certain assets and property, and a cash summary would disclose very little about the true finances and net worth of the organisation.

These larger clubs, societies and associations, at their annual general meetings, present to their members an income and expenditure account together with a balance sheet on the lines we already know. The long-sounding term 'income and expenditure account' is only another name for the profit and loss account with which we are familiar. Profit and loss would not, of course, be appropriate terminology for a non-profit oriented organisation. Similarly the 'capital' becomes the 'accumulated fund' or occasionally 'general reserve'. Clubs and societies may also, for their own convenience, split their reserves into other categories; for example, a 'maintenance reserve' into which sums are transferred each year to meet periodic maintenance bills such as redecorating.

Often an examination question presents the candidate with a receipts and payments account (or simply a summarised cash book, which is the same thing) and, subject to a number of adjustments, requires an income and expenditure account to be made up together with a balance sheet.

An illustration of a typical examination problem is now given.

The Heathside Tennis Club
Receipts and Payments Account for the year ended 31 October

	£		£
Balance 1 Nov.	97.20	Postages/stationery	37.80
Subs. rec'd (including		Refreshments bought	124.40
£30 in advance)	920.00	Dance expenses	70.40
Dance proceeds (gross)	137.00	New nets	460.00
Donations	50.00	General expenses	25.20
Receipts from teas		Wages of groundsman	612.00
and socials	244.60	Heating/lighting, etc.	83.40
		Balance c/d	35.60
	1448.80		1448.80
Balance b/d	35.60		

In making up the annual accounts as at 31 October for presentation to club members, the following information is to be taken into account:

The club's assets and property on 1 November, one year ago:

Clubhouse at original cost	£3000.00
Nets/equipment at book value	260.00
Stock of tinned drinks, etc.	43.00
Cash on hand (see cash summary)	97.20

There were no arrears of subscriptions one year ago, and all expense creditors had been paid.

Certain adjustments are now to be taken into account in making up the income and expenditure account and the balance sheet:

(a) invoice for electricity £22.80 unpaid at 31 October

(b) subscriptions in arrears at 31 October amounted to £50

(c) subscriptions in advance £30 (shown in cash summary)

(*d*) wages owing to groundsman at 31 October £24
(*e*) stock of refreshments at end of current season £49.60
(*f*) nets/equipment account to be depreciated by £200.

The first stage of the answer to this problem is to find the commencing capital (sometimes called the **accumulated fund**), and then make up the subscriptions account to find the true income from members for the year.

	clubhouse	£3000.00
Accumulated	nets/equipt.	260.00
fund	stock 1 Nov.	43.00
	cash balance 1 Nov.	97.20 £3400.20

Naturally, any liabilities at the beginning of the year would have been deducted from this amount of £3400.20, but in this instance there were no liabilities.

Dr. **Subscriptions Account** Cr.

Oct.		£	Oct.		£
31	Subs. paid in advance by members c/d	30.00	31	Actual receipts as per cash summary	920.00
31	Transfer to Income & Expd. a/c	940.00	31	Subs. owing by members c/d	50.00
		970.00			97.00
Nov.			Nov.		
1	Debtors for subs. b/d	50.00	1	Creditors for subs. b/d	30.00

Subscriptions taken to the income and expenditure account must show the actual income from members for the year.

The final accounts of the club can now be made up on these lines:

Income and Expenditure Statement – year ended 31 October

	£	£	£	Last year's figures
Income				
Subscriptions		940.00		
Donations		50.00		
Gross receipts from dances, teas, etc.	381.60			
Adjustment on stocks	6.60			
	388.20			
Less dance & catering expenses	194.80	193.40	1183.40	
Expenditure				
Postages/stationery		37.80		
Groundsman's wages	612.00			
Wages owing at 31 Oct.	24.00	636.00		
Heating/lighting	83.40			
Electricity owing	22.80	106.20		
General expenses		25.20		
		805.20		
Deprec. nets/equipt. a/c		200.00	1005.20	
Surplus to accumulated fund			£178.20	

Balance Sheet of The Heathside Tennis Club as at 31 October

	£	£	£	Last year's figures
Fixed assets				
Clubhouse at cost		3000.00		
Nets/equipment	260.00			
Additions	460.00			
	720.00			
Less depreciation	200.00	520.00	3520.00	
Current assets				
Stock of refreshments		49.60		
Debtors for subscriptions		50.00		
Cash in hand		35.60	135.20	
			£3655.20	
Capital and liabilities		£		
Accumulated fund 1 Nov.		3400.20		
Add surplus income		178.20	3578.40	
Current liabilities				
Subscriptions in advance		30.00		
Creditors for wages		24.00		
Creditors for electricity		22.80	76.80	
			£3655.20	

Assignments

KEY POINTS

1 Note that the vertical style of revenue statement has been adopted in the text, although occasionally the old horizontal style will be found, where treasurers are simply following the previous year's layout.

2 In all problems involving income and expenditure, first establish the *closing cash balance* needed for the final balance sheet. Also make up a subscriptions account, or work out the subscriptions by arithmetic.

3 Sometimes a club has a small bar and/or offers catering facilities to members. A short trading account is then made up in the ordinary way, and the profit or loss on trading is carried down to a general income and expenditure account.

4 Do not confuse subscriptions in advance with rates in advance. If club members have paid subscriptions in advance, they become creditors of the club; if their subscriptions are in arrears, they are debtors of the club.

27.1 Make up a receipts and payments account from this information listed by the treasurer of a small local dramatic society at 31 December.

	£
Opening cash/bank balances (combined)	115.50
Subscriptions actually received from members during the year	150.00
Donations received	25.00
Net receipts from rehearsals/socials etc.	14.80
Ticket sales on productions	280.60
Rent of local hall	130.00
Stamps/stationery	6.20
Purchase of reading material and plays	84.50
Payment of royalties	62.00
Lighting/heating	28.70
Refreshments and drinks bought	92.40
Honorarium to treasurer 31 December	10.00

27.2 The cash book of the White Collar Workers' Association was analysed in total as follows: subscriptions from members £860; donations received £430; sundry receipts £175; rates paid £120; furniture bought £270; salaries paid £600; fees to lecturers £250; general expenses £210. Cash balance 1 January £30.

The Association owned its own premises shown at cost of £4000. The old furniture had been given to the Red Cross and written off the previous year. The position with regard to out-standings at the year-end was as follows:

Subs. owing at 1 Jan. £46; and at 31 Dec. £66. Creditors for stationery £76 at the beginning of the year, and £24 at the end.

Take the valuation of stationery unused at £54, and make up an income and expenditure account and a balance sheet at 31 December. A payment of £130 for stationery by the association was found by the auditors to be debited to general expenses.

28

CONTROL ACCOUNTS

Self-balancing ledgers

A control account is a convenient device used as a check upon the arithmetical accuracy of postings to a particular ledger or section of ledgers. In the latter case the system is sometimes called **sectional balancing**. Before computers were available to make such calculations and checks almost instantaneously, this was a very important safeguard.

The term **self-balancing** refers to the inclusion of a control account, kept normally at the front or at the back of a ledger, and used as a check by the ledger clerk on the total of his balances extracted from that ledger.

In addition to providing a check on the work of the book-keeper, self- or sectional balancing is also an aid to any internal audit system in force.

The bank cash book

The control accounts themselves are merely *summaries of totals taken from other books*, in the main from the books of original entry. The rulings in these books of prime entry are adapted to suit the needs of the particular business and the control system adopted.

The bank cash book is a feature of the control system. The bank and discount columns are still used, but the old cash columns are replaced by 'details' columns. *All receipts*, cash and cheques, are *banked daily*, and all payments shown in the main cash book are *made by cheque*, leaving the small routine cash disbursements to be paid by the petty cashier. The total wages paid each week will be met by a cheque cashed for that purpose, and the salaried employees will be paid monthly by credit transfer from their employer to their own bank accounts.

The debit and credit details columns are extended in analysis form to provide the information required by the ledger clerks for their control summaries. For example, the cumulative total of the payments from debtors provides control with the total amount credited to all the customers' accounts in the sales ledger. Similarly all payments to suppliers are listed in one particular column on the credit side of the cash book, to establish the total amount paid to trade creditors during the period.

The general principles of control are best explained by simple illustration. In this example, we are concerned only with transactions on the sales side of the business, the credit sales to customers during one month, their payments on account of goods they have bought, discounts allowed to them and credits for goods returned. The purpose of the control account is to prove the arithmetical accuracy of the total of the debtors' balances extracted by the sales ledger clerk on 31 July.

Illustration

The ledger accounts of only four credit customers are given for the month of July.

Smith

July		£	July		£
1	Balance	100	8	Cash	95
10	SDB	120		disct.	5
			12	SRB	15

Jones

July		£	July		£
1	Balance	50	18	Cash	48
20	SDB	75		disct.	2
			22	SRB	5

Robinson

July		£	July		£
1	Balance	20	25	Cash	19
				disct.	1

Brown

July		£	July		£
22	SDB	10	24	Cash	10
31	SDB	3			

The bank cash book (debit or receipts side only) is shown in brief detail, followed by the other books of original entry on the sales side, the sales day book and the returns inwards book.

		Fol.	Disc.	Sales ledger	Cash sales	Sundries	Bank
			£	£	£	£	£
July 1	Balance b/f					400	400
8	Smith	SL	5	95			95
12	Cash sales	NL			80		80
18	Jones	SL	2	48			
	Cash sales	NL			30		78
24	Brown	SL		10			
25	Robinson	SL	1	19			29
31	Cash sales	NL			40		40
			—	—	—	—	—
			8	172	150	400	722

Sales Day Book

July			£
10	Smith	SL	120
20	Jones	SL	75
22	Brown	SL	10
31	Brown	SL	3
			208

Sales Returns Book

July			£
12	Smith	SL	15
22	Jones	SL	5
			—
			20

Again it is emphasised that this small illustration concerns only sales control, in connection with the items and transactions affecting the sales or debtors' ledger only.

At the month end, the sales ledger clerk will extract the credit customers' balances, listing them as follows:

	£
Smith	105
Jones	70
Brown	3
to give the total	£178 owing by debtors

The sales clerk then proves the accuracy of the postings to the sales ledger by making up the control account, either at the front or at the back of the sales ledger. This account contains the summaries and totals *made up by other employees* in the firm, the figures being extracted from the bank cash book, the sales day book and the returns inwards book. The control account made up by the sales ledger clerk is called the **general ledger control account**, made up on these lines:

General Ledger Control Account for July

July			£	July			£
31	Sales returns	SRB	20	1	Balance b/f		170
31	Total payments			31	Total sales for		
	received	CB	172		month of July	SDB	208
	& discount allowed	CB	8				
31	Balance c/d		178				
			378				378
				August			
				1	Balance b/d		178

The commencing *credit* balance of the above control account (£170) is the sum total of the debtors' balances at the beginning of the month, 1 July. Note that the totals shown within this control account are on the reverse side to the individual items that are already posted to this ledger. There is always a *credit* balance on the control account kept in the sales ledger, generally referred to as the general ledger control account (in effect a contra account to the sales ledger control account kept in the general ledger mentioned in the next paragraph).

In another section of the accounting department, the clerk responsible for the posting up of the general ledger also makes up a separate control account to prove this accounts section's postings on the general ledger and expense side. That part of the new control relating to the sales side of the business is called the sales ledger control account. It starts with the commencing debit balance of £170 and finishes with the total for the sales ledger balances of £178, and is an additional check on both the postings to the sales ledger and to the general ledger.

The purchase ledger control follows a similar procedure to that briefly outlined on the sales side, except that again, of course, it will be in reverse of the sales procedure as already illustrated.

Pause for thought

'Errors in balancing were numerous some years ago. Self-balancing ledger have helped the book-keeper and the auditor a great deal.' Explain this statement and consider how the complete control system of a business has developed from total accounts and the self-balancing and sectional ledgers which were first put to use.

Assignments

KEY POINTS

1 The main difficulty experienced by students is knowing either the heading of the control account or the correct side for their sales and purchases debits and credits, etc.
First make sure of the ledger in which the account is to be written up.

If it is the sales ledger, all totals will be in reverse (on the control account) to the actual items shown on the individual debtors' accounts.

If it is the purchases ledger, again reverse the items on the control account, to the various postings within the bought ledger.

2 Note any mention of bad debts refers to the sales ledger. Bad debts are always shown on the same side as debtors' payments and discount allowed.

3 Note also that small debit balances in BL and small credit balances in SL at the end of month must be shown *above and below the totals* when making up control accounts.

4 Be careful with transfers between ledgers, increasing the debit in one ledger and decreasing the credit in another – and vice versa.

28.1 Prepare the purchase ledger control account (as drawn up by the general ledger clerk) for the month of January and carry down the balance.

Jan.		£
1	Credit balances	30 884
	Debit balances	122
31	Purchases for month	41 350
	Paid to suppliers (cheques)	26 440
	Discounts received	586
	Small credit balances paid out of petty cash	45
	Returns outward	958
	Contras settling small debits	82
	Debit balances at month end	40

28.2 From the balances below you are required to make up th
purchase and the sales ledger control accounts as they woul
appear at the back of their respective ledgers:

June		£
1	Bought ledger balances	2 433
	Sales ledger balances	3 486
30	Purchases for month	9 295
	Sales for month	13 840
	Paid to suppliers	7 616
	Discounts received	190
	Returns inwards	168
	Received from customers	12 327
	Discounts allowed	255
	Returns outward	177
	Bad debts written off	36
	Bills receivable	585
	Bills payable	480
	Dishonoured cheque of customer	42
	Debit balances transferred from sales ledger to bought ledger	58

28.3 Draft your own ruling of a bank cash book for both receipts an
payments. Make a number of entries useful for a control system
in force, and take the totals of your columns to a control accoun
made up for this purpose. Complete this same control accoun
with the day book and returns book totals for the same period.

29
PARTNERSHIP ACCOUNTS

The ordinary book-keeping records of a partnership are kept exactly on the same lines as those of a sole trader. The cash book, the day books, and the customers' and suppliers' ledgers are posted up in the same way as that already shown. The net profit of the business is ascertained in the same way as before, but, because there are now two or more owners of the business, the proportion of profit entitlement have to be worked out separately.

The appropriation account

Since the trading profit is to be divided, not necessarily equally, the profit and loss section of the main revenue account is extended by a third appendage called the **appropriation account**. The trading profit for the period is split in the appropriation account, and divided according to the terms laid down by the partnership agreement or contract. *In the absence of any written or typed agreement, or by implied custom of the past, partners are presumed to share profits and losses equally*, irrespective of the size of their capital accounts or their holding of partnership assets. This is laid down in the Partnership Act of 1890.

Separate capital accounts

Partners' capital accounts have no direct bearing on their profit-sharing ratios, unless there are specific terms laid down to the contrary. The senior partner may have a capital of £8000 and the junior a capital o £2000 and yet their written agreement or past custom may indicat that their profit sharing ratios are three-fifths and two-fifths.

Interest on capital

Interest is sometimes allowed as a form of compensation for those part ners with larger financial holdings in the firm. This interest is a charg against the net trading profit before its division between the partners the double entry being a debit to appropriation and a credit to the individual current accounts of the partners.

Current accounts

This is a new term applicable to the private accounts of partners within the firm, not to be confused with the ordinary bank current account A partner's current account replaces the old drawings account of the sole trader. The total drawings of the individual partner is debited to that partner's current account; the share of profit and also any interest on capital or any partnership salary to which the partner is entitled are credited to the account.

It is customary to keep fixed capital accounts of all partners quite separate and distinct from the individual current accounts of each partner.

Illustration

Ned and Fred are in partnership with capitals of £4000 and £2000 respectively. Their partnership agreement states that the net trading profits will be shared in the proportions of three-quarters and one-quarter, but that Fred should be credited with a partnership salary of £1000 a year before the final allocation of net trading profit. In addition, interest on capital of 10% per annum is to be credited to the current account of each partner. The net trading profit for the year under review, ended 31 December, was £13 600.

The credit balances of the partners' current accounts brought forward were: Ned £120 and Fred £80; the partners' drawings for the year were: Ned £9350 and Fred £4220. At the balance sheet date Fred had not yet withdrawn any part of his salary for the current year.

Show the appropriation account of the firm, the partners' capital and current accounts (as they would appear in the private ledger), and draft the capital and liabilities side of the balance sheet as at 31 December.

Profit and Loss Appropriation Account

	£		£
Interest on capital		Net trading profit	
Ned	400	b/d	13 600
Fred	200		
Salary of Fred	1 000		
Shares of profit			
Ned	9 000		
Fred	3 000		
	13 600		13 600

Dr.   **Capital Accounts** (fixed original balances)   Cr.

		Ned	Fred				Ned	Fred
				Jan. 1	b/f		£4000	£2000

Dr.   **Current Accounts**   Cr.

		Ned £	Fred £			Ned £	Fred £
Dec. 31	Drawings	9350	4220	Jan. 1	Balances b/f	120	80
31	Balances c/d	170	60	Dec. 31	Int. on capital	400	200
					Salary		1000
					Shares of profit	9000	3000
		9520	4280			9520	4280
				Jan. 1	Balances b/d	170	60

Balance Sheet of Ned and Fred
as at 31 December

Capital and liabilities section		
Capital accounts	£	£
Ned	4000	
Fred	2000	6000
Current accounts		
Ned: Balance 1 Jan.	120	
Int. on capital	400	
Share of profit	9000	
	9520	
Less drawings	9350	170
Fred: Balance 1 Jan.	80	
Int. on capital	200	
Salary	1000	
Share of profit	3000	
	4280	
Less drawings	4220	60
Current liabilities		—

Partners' salary

In the illustration just shown Fred has been credited with his full salary of £1000 (on his current account) *because it has not yet been paid*. He becomes a creditor of his own firm for the time being. When the salary is withdrawn, cash will be credited and his current account debited. If Fred had withdrawn part of his salary (on account) prior to the balance sheet date, the double entry would have been a credit to cash and a debit to partnership salaries account, with *no credit appearing on Fred's current account for that part of the salary already withdrawn.*

Amalgamation of sole traders

Occasionally, two or more sole traders decide to amalgamate their respective businesses and become partners. The book-keeping entries in connection with the presentation of the balance sheet of the new firm are simple enough providing the capital account of *each sole trader is adjusted*, according to the terms agreed upon by the prospective partners, *before any attempt is made to draft a final balance sheet for the new firm.*

Illustration

Ellen and Emily are cousins with small retail drapery shops, both rented, in the town centre of Hereford. They decide to become partners and save a considerable sum on competitive advertising and also on bulk buying. The date of their amalgamation is to be 1 April. Their last individual balance sheets are now shown at 31 March in the older 'T' style of presentation.

Ellen's Balance Sheet as at 31 March

	£		£
Capital	5800	Fittings/fixtures	1500
Creditors	450	Van at cost	1250
Bank overdraft	250	Stock of goods	2200
		Trade debtors	1550
	£6500		£6500

Emily's Balance Sheet as at 31 March

	£		£
Capital	6460	Furniture/fittings	750
Trade creditors	840	Tools/equipment	1320
		Stock	1840
		Trade debtors	2880
		Bank	510
	£7300		£7300

The partnership agreement of the new firm states that profits and losses are to be shared equally as from 1 April, and that certain amendments and adjustments are to be made to some of the asset values as shown on the two balance sheets dated 31 March, namely:

All furniture, fittings, etc., are to be reduced by 20% of their book value; the van is to be revalued at £800, and tools/equipment at £1000. Provisions are to be made against possible bad debts of 10% of the trade debtors' balances. Miss Ellen is to repay her bank overdraft privately, and the bank account of Miss Emily is to be taken over by the new firm. The stock on hand shown in each balance sheet is to be depreciated by 25%.

Answer

First of all re-draft the individual balance sheets of the sole traders at 31 March, subject to the partnership terms agreed upon.

	Ellen £	Emily £		Ellen £	Emily £
Capital accounts	4595	5242	Fittings/fixtures	1200	600
Trade creditors	450	840	Van	800	
			Tools/equipment		1000
			Stock	1650	1380
			Debtors *less* prov. for bad debts	1395	2592
			Bank		510
	5045	6082		5045	6082

The balance sheet for the new firm as at 1 April can now quickly be drafted by lumping together the figures shown above.

Balance Sheet of Ellen and Emily as at 1 April

		£	£
Assets employed			
Fixed assets			
Fittings/fixtures		1800	
Tools/equipment		1000	
Van at valuation		800	3600
Current assets			
Stock on hand		3030	
Trade debtors	4430		
Less provision	443	3987	
Bank		510	7527
			11127
Financed by			
Capital accounts			
Ellen		4595	
Emily		5242	9837
Current liabilities			
Trade creditors			1290
			11127

Overdrawn current account

A partner who overdraws on the current account becomes a debtor to the firm. The current account shows, temporarily, a debit balance, and at the balance sheet date, must be switched over to the bottom of the listed assets. However, it would be ignored in calculating the working capital of the business.

Interest on drawings

Interest is sometimes charged on partners' drawings with a view to curbing heavy and frequent withdrawals on the firm's bank account. This interest on drawings is debited to the partners' individual current accounts in addition to the sums withdrawn, and is credited to the firm's appropriation account as a small gain to the business.

For example, if the senior partner of a professional firm, by agreement, withdraws £2000 at the end of each quarter, subject to an interest charge of 8% per annum, the individual debits to her current account for a year would be calculated in this manner:

			£
31 March	(interest 1 April–31 December) 9 months at 8%	=	120
30 June	(interest 1 July–31 Dec.) 6 months at 8%	=	80
30 Sept.	(interest 1 Oct.–31 Dec.) 3 months at 8%	=	40
31 Dec.	(last day of trading year – no charge)		—
			£240

This total of £240 would be credited to the firm's appropriation account at the end of the trading year, and the amount of £8240 (£8000 drawings plus £240 interest) would be debited to this particular partner's current account.

Goodwill in accounts

Goodwill has been defined as 'the likelihood that the old customers will continue to deal with the old firm' and as 'the benefit arising from connection and reputation'.

Occasionally there appears at the top of the fixed assets on a balance sheet the descriptive term 'Goodwill £___'. It looks impressive, particularly if it is a large amount, but actually it does not mean very much beyond the fact that a debit balance for this intangible asset is still being carried forward in the books. This debit balance is a paper entry from the past (probably created when the business last changed hands or when a new partner was admitted to the old firm). It is an intangible asset; you cannot see or touch it, and its value is indeterminable until the business is sold or there is a change in the ownership. Even on the sale of the business, the value of goodwill, as part of the purchase price asked by the vendor, is always problematical and subject to much discussion and deliberation before the final price is agreed upon by the new owner.

A new business has no goodwill. It has to be earned and developed. As the business expands, its connection and reputation increases, so that when it is sold or a change of ownership takes place the valuation of the business 'as a going concern' is worth substantially more than the listed value of its net assets and property. *The difference in value between the net assets and the actual purchase price is the goodwill of the business.*

Illustration

Sam Brown has rented a corner shop in the suburbs for the past twenty years. He is now retiring, and his last balance sheet, dated 30 June, is shown below on the left. It has been checked over by George Smith, who agrees the vendor's price of £18 000 for the business, advertised with 'all assets and property to be taken over at balance sheet figures, and the trade creditors to be settled by the new owner'.

Balance Sheet of Sam Brown, vendor, as at 30 June

Assets and property	£	£
Fixed assets		
Van at valuation	1 950	
Fittings/equipt.	7 800	9 750
Current assets		
Stock at 30 June	2 800	
Trade debtors	450	3 250
		13 000
Financed by		
Capital: S. Brown	£	
Balance 1 July	14 000	
Net profit for year	5 500	
	19 500	
Less drawings	7 500	12 000
Current liabilities		
Trade creditors	1 000	
		£13 000

Balance Sheet of George Smith, purchaser, as at 1 July

Assets and property	£	£
Fixed assets		
Goodwill at cost	6 000	
Van at valuation	1 950	
Fittings/equipt.	7 800	15 750
Current assets		
Stock at 1 July	2 800	
Trade debtors	450	3 250
		19 000
Financed by		
Capital: G. Smith		£
Balance 1 July		18 000
Current liabilities		
Trade creditors		1 000
		£19 000

Comparing the two balance sheets it will be seen that George Smith has acquired the whole of the assets and liabilities of Sam Brown at their valuation at 30 June, and, in the agreed purchase price of £18 000 has, in effect, paid a premium of £6000 in acquiring these assets. The capital account of the new owner thus becomes £18 000, the price he has paid for his new business. The excess amount paid over and above the valuation of net assets taken over (i.e. £6000) is debited to the goodwill account, and on his first balance sheet dated 1 July, is taken to the top of the fixed assets. This intangible asset, though only a paper entry, is a debit balance in the accounting records of George Smith, and will continue to be shown at the top of his assets on future balance sheets, unless he decides to reduce or write off part of the debit through appropriations of good years of profit.

Sometimes, too, where a new partner is being admitted to an existing firm, the old partner(s) create a goodwill account, perhaps only temporarily, by debiting an agreed figure, say £10 000, to a new asset account headed goodwill, crediting amounts to their capital (or current) accounts in the proportions they previously shared profits and losses, shown in this way by journal entry:

Dec. 31		£	£
	Goodwill account	10000	
	Capital accounts:		
	A		6000
	B		4000
Goodwill account created on admission of C, credited to capital accounts of A and B in their old profit sharing ratios.			

The creation of a goodwill account provides some compensation for the past work and effort of the old partners. It often relieves the new incoming partner from finding a fairly substantial sum on admission to the firm, although generally he would still be expected to bring in a small introductory capital.

There is no hard and fast rule laid down for the valuation of goodwill. Some of the small retail traders might adopt a goodwill valuation of ten times the average gross weekly takings, with property, stock etc. at a separate valuation. Professional firms such as accountants and solicitors sometimes require double their annual gross fees or perhaps three times their net fees (average net profits over recent years).

Since the goodwill debit is simply an arbitrary figure used as an adjustment on business valuation perhaps a long time ago, often bearing no relationship to the present-day true worth of the business, it is advisable to write down its book value out of profits as early as possible, in this way strengthening the reserves or perhaps substituting genuine fixed assets in lieu.

Accounting standards may also require non-purchased goodwill (and indeed purchased goodwill) to be written off immediately or over a period of time. The creation of goodwill in the accounts of a partnership can also cause capital gains tax problems, which is why it is normally written off again immediately, rather than being carried forward.

Assignments

KEY POINTS

1   In the absence of written agreement or laid-down policy or custom, Section 24 of the *Partnership Act* of 1890 states that partnership profits and losses will be shared equally.

2   Appropriations and charges against trading profit such as interest on capital and partnership salaries are debited to the appropriation account before final distribution of profit.

3   When two or more sole traders amalgamate to become partners, revalue and adjust their capitals separately *before* making any attempt to lump together the joint assets/ liabilities of the new firm.

4   Partnership salaries are debited *in full* against the firm's trading profit. If part of salary is not paid, it will be shown as a credit on individual partner's current account.

5   Adjustment of profit-sharing ratios.

A and B share profits 2:1. They admit their chief clerk to take one-fifth of the profits; the old partners still to maintain their previous ratios.

The new profit-sharing ratios:
C, the new partner, will take one-fifth of the profit, leaving four-fifths between A and B.
A will take ⅔ of ⅘ths = ⁸⁄₁₅ths
B will take ⅓ of ⅘ths = ⁴⁄₁₅ths
Thus the ratios of the new firm will be: 8:4:3.

29.1 Make up the appropriation account and the partner's current accounts from the information given below.

	Capitals £	Current a/cs £	Drawings £
Melon	4000	250 Cr.	6500
Lemon	2000	100 Dr.	6800

Lemon is to be credited half-yearly with a salary of £500. Each partner is to be credited with 8% per annum interest on capital. The net trading profit for six months ended 30 June was £14 500.

29.2 A, B and C share profits in the ratios of 3:2:1. Net trading for this year is £12 000 after charging C's salary in full. Interest on capital is allowed at 10%. Make up the partners' current accounts on the balance sheet at 31 December.

Cash Book

Jan. 1	Capital a/cs		£	June 30	½ yearly		£
	A		5000		salary of C		500
	B		4000	Dec.			
	C		3000	31	Drawings		
					A		4800
					B		3500
					C		2500

29.3 Sue Pugh's assets and liabilities at 30 June are listed:

fittings £8000; bank overdraft £550; stock £1800; trade creditors £1750; trade debtors £1200.

She takes her friend May Day into partnership as from 1 July. Miss Day pays the sum of £2000 into the firm's bank account, and also brings in her own car (valued at £1500 and some useful equipment valued at £200).

The partnership agreement provides for interest on capital at 6% per annum, and the profit sharing ratios of the new firm are to be:

Miss Pugh, two-thirds.
Miss Day, one-third.

You are required to make up the balance sheet of the partnership as at 1 July.

REVISION EXERCISE 5

1   The Overlanders' Club was established ten years ago for social and recreational purposes, in particular travel abroad. The secretary of the club prepared the following summary of the cash book transactions for the year ended 31 March.

	£		£
Balance (cash and bank		Furniture bought	120
combined	804	Catering expenses	266
Subscriptions received	915	Repairs/maintenance	15
Donations received	28	Rent of rooms	180
Receipts from socials,		Wages of temporary staff	620
raffles, etc.	384	Lighting/heating	88
		Books/magazines	76
		Printing and stationery	22

The club rents two large rooms overlooking the park at the economic annual rent of £240, paid quarterly, the landlord paying the rates. Fixtures and fittings on the last balance sheet stood at £680. The committee decided to revalue this at £650, including the additions bought earlier in the year.

Books and magazines were regarded as expendable, to be treated purely as revenue.

The position with regard to members' subscriptions was:

1 April (beginning of year):	subscriptions owing £44
	subscriptions in advance £28
31 March (end of the year):	subscriptions owing £56
	subscriptions in advance £24

A catering account of £35 was owing on 31 March; £16 was due to the Midland Electricity Board and £12 owing for wages.

From the above information, you are required to make up the income and expenditure account of the club and a blance sheet as at 31 March.

2 Janetta Meade and Philippa Richmond are in partnership sharing profits and losses in the proportions two-thirds and one-third. Interest at 6% is allowed on capital and Miss Richmond is entitled to a partnership salary of £400 a year before the profits are apportioned. Draw up the final accounts of the partnership from the trial balance and adjustments below:

Trial Balance   31 December

	£	£
Capital accounts 1 Jan.		
J.M.		7 000
P.R.		4 500
Current accounts J.M.		120
P.R.	45	
Partners' drawings J.M.	2 800	
P.R.	1 700	
Partnership salaries	200	
Purchases/sales	5 600	16 750
Returns inwards/outwards	40	70
Wages & NIC	2200	
Carriage outward	120	
Provision for bad debts		105
Trade debtors/creditors	2 400	1 250
Machinery (less depreciation)	7 650	
Depreciation for year	850	
Fittings and equipment at cost	460	
Lighting/heating	330	
Office salaries & NIC	1 600	
Stock 1 Jan.	1 500	
Warehousing expenses	230	
Advertising	400	
Rent, rates and insurance	960	
Bad debts	85	
Cash and bank balances	705	
Discounts allowed/received	325	455
	30 250	30 250

(a) Stock on hand 31 December £1820
(b) Rates paid in advance to 31 March £100
(c) Provision for debtors to be maintained at 5%
(d) Wages owing at 31 December £25
(e) Carry forward £200 already paid on advertising account.

30

ACCOUNTING FOR MANAGEMENT

Figures belong to the 'counting house', the province of the accountant. Management is more interested in their significance, in the story they have to tell.

Simplicity of presentation is as important as accuracy. Revenue accounts should show not only the ultimate calculation of profit or loss, but also how the results have been achieved. Balance sheets should be presented so that the non-accountant can interpret the figures.

If they have not already done so, most students at this stage adapt their trading account to show the cost of sales figures, thus:

		£			£
Stock 1 June		1000	Sales for month	£6500	
Purchases for month	£2200		Less returns	100	6400
Less returns	50	2150			
		3150			
Stock 30 June		850			
		2300			
Production wages		1800			
Warehousing expenses		120			
Cost of sales		4220			
Gross profit c/d		2180			
		6400			6400

By way of comparison, the smaller statement shown next is even more informative with less detail to absorb, and would be easier to understand by the non-accountant.

Net sales for the month of June		£6400
Cost of sales		
Materials consumed	£2300	
Production wages	1800	
Warehousing expenses	120	4220
	Gross profit	£2180

We could also group the various losses and expense items of the old-style profit and loss account in a manner which would mean something more to the casual observer, thus:

	£	£
		£
Gross trading profit		2180
Distribution expenses	£	
Carriage (outwards)	25	
Van repairs	36	
Petrol and oil	23	
Depreciation of vans	65	149
Selling expenses		
Advertising	52	
Postages (proportion)	14	66
Office and administration		
Salaries	490	
Telephone	44	
Insurance	18	
Printing/stationery	33	
Postages (proportion)	28	613
Financial		
Discounts	30	
Depreciation office equipment	20	50
Total expenses		878
Net profit before tax		£1302

For comparative purposes, the figures for the previous year could be shown in the marginal space on the right. Sometimes, too, each item of expense is calculated as a percentage of net sales.

To present final accounts in narrative form, the trial balance can be made up on these lines, *after all adjustments* have been dealt with and the cost of sales figures ascertained:

Trial Balance   30 June

	£	£
Fixed assets		
Premises at cost	6 000	
Van (book balance)	300	
Current assets		
Stock 30 June	1 230	
Trade debtors	1 300	
Rates in advance	80	
Cash/bank	520	
Loan capital		
10% mortgage on premises		2 000
Current liabilities		
Trade creditors		600
Expense creditors		40
Interest due on mortgage		200
Claims of proprietorship		4 000
Capital owned		
Revenue income		
Net sales		12 760
Revenue expenditure		
Cost of sales	6 500	
Salaries & NIC	2 200	
Office expenses	630	
Advertising	220	
Van expenses	50	
Rates and insurance	270	
Mortgage interest	200	
Depreciation of van	100	
	19 600	19 600

Note that the inclusion of the cost of sales figure on the trial balance
means that stocks and purchases have already been adjusted to
arrive at the total debit of £6500. In consequence, the stock figure of
£1230 on the trial balance is that of the closing stock of 30 June. Note
also that the van account shows the up-to-date balance, after the
adjustment for depreciation, and that the mortgage interest, being
due and not yet paid, is shown both as a debit (to be charged to
revenue) and also as a credit (under current liabilities).

Revenue Account for the month of June

		£	Previous year
Net sales for the month		12 760	
	£		
Costs of sales		6 500	
Selling/distribution			
Advertising	£220		
Van expenses	50		
Depreciation of van	100	370	
Office/administration			
Salaries & NIC	£2 200		
Office and general	630		
Rates and insurance	270	3 100	
Financial expense			
Mortgage	200	10 170	
	Net trading profit for month	£2 590	

The vertical narrative style of presentation, for both the revenue account and the balance sheet, has been adopted generally throughout the commercial world. In particular, this new format, with its many explanatory footnotes for greater ease in interpretation, lends itself to the final accounts of limited companies. It is shown in further detail in Chapter 35.

The balance sheet in this illustration is shown overleaf, but since it refers in this instance to the accounts of a sole trader, note that there is a certain paucity of detail, on the capital side, when compared with the balance sheet of a limited company.

Note that in this illustration the proprietor's capital account has been made up to date at 30 June, presumably after deduction of any drawings for the month, but before the addition of the net trading profit. The term 'retained profit' would not be suitable in this instance. The proprietor may have some good reason for not disclosing withdrawals from the business, and, in any event, is not subject to the strict procedure and regulations of the Companies Acts.

Dulance Sheet as at 30 June

Assets employed		£	£
Fixed assets			
Premises at cost		6000	
Van, *less* depreciation		300	6300
Current assets	£		
Stock 30 June	1230		
Trade debtors	1300		
Payment in advance	80		
Cash/bank	520	3130	
Current liabilities			
Trade creditors	600		
Expense creditors	40		
Mortgage interest	200	840	
Working capital			2290
			8590
Financed by		£	£
Proprietary capital			
Balance 30 June		4000	
Net trading profit		2590	6590
Fixed liability			
10% Mortgage loan			
(secured on premises)			2000
			8590

Assignments

30.1 What is meant by the statement 'Figures belong to the "counting house"' and why is management likely to be more interested in the real story they have to tell?

30.2 Comparative figures are given of the average stock, the stock-turn, and the mark-up cost of two distinct businesses. Through the medium of gross profit percentages indicate which, in your opinion, is apparently the most successful business.

	Average stock	Stock-turn	Mark-up on cost
	£		
Business A	3500	6 times in the year	35%
Business B	3500	10 times in the year	22½%

30.3 Edwina and Selina Black are equal partners in a gown shop, bought fifteen years ago, with financial help provided by Edwina's husband in the first instance, and he still has a priority claim upon the net assets of their retail venture. The last balance sheet of the firm is now shown.

Balance Sheet of E. and S. Black as at 30 June

	£	£
Assets employed		
Fixed assets		
Goodwill	5 000	
Premises at cost	8 000	
Fixtures/fittings at cost	1 500	
Motor van at valuation	1 250	15 750
Current assets		
Stock	1 480	
Trade debtors	2 340	
Insurance in advance	65	
Cash in hand	15	3 900
Current account S. Black		350
		£20 000
Financed by		
Partners' capital		
Edwina Black	2 000	
Selina Black	2 000	4 000
Current account E. Black		240
Mortgage loan Ian Black		10 000
(secured on premises)		
Current liabilities		
Bank overdraft	1 400	
Trade creditors	4 000	
Expense creditors	360	5 760
		£20 000

Discuss or give your views upon the following points with regard to this balance sheet.

(a) At first glance, does this appear to be a good business?

(b) Say last year's net profit was £15 000 divisible between the two sisters. Would this be a good return on the capital finance?

(c) What is the working capital of this business? Why is the current account of one partner on the assets side?

(d) If the bank and the trade creditors insisted upon early or immediate repayment of their debts, how could the business survive?

31
COSTS OF PRODUCTION AND MANUFACTURING ACCOUNTS

— Measurement of working capital —

Working capital is profitable only when fully employed. When a merchanting business regularly carries a huge bank balance, the bank probably makes far more money out of that current asset than the business owner.

Banks use money to create money. The trader or merchant, too, can make good use of surplus money in a variety of ways, such as buying reserve commodity stocks in economic markets, obtaining maximum discounts from suppliers, purchasing up-to-date machinery and equipment, and extending the market scope through wider publicity. In the inflationary markets of today, money wisely spent now is more profitable than money used in six months' time.

Minimum cash cover must, of course, be available for both routine purposes and possible contingencies, so a certain degree of liquidity is important. This means that a close and constant watch must be kept on the amount of working capital and its most profitable allocation between current assets and current liabilities.

The regular and systematic measurement of working capital has become a general function of the accountant and the financial director. Certain arithmetical devices are used to measure liquidity, including various ratios such as stock to sales, debtors to sales, current assets to current liabilities, and quick assets to current liabilities, the latter commonly known as the **acid test ratio** dealt with in Chapter 19.

——— Prime cost and oncost ———

A manufacturer must buy raw material and allow for all manner of huge labour and factory costs long before selling the finished product, sometimes weeks, perhaps months afterwards. Meanwhile, that same manufacturer probably has to borrow money at a high rate of interest to maintain production.

Prime cost is the term used for the direct expenses of production – the materials, labour and the actual expenses that can be definitely allocated to certain production schedules. In addition, the manufacturer incurs many other expenses that cannot, as a rule, be allocated easily to a particular job or contract. These expenses include the rent and rates of the factory, lighting and heating, factory power, the wages of supervisors, time-keepers and greasers, and the wear and tear (depreciation) of the factory plant. These necessary and essential expenses of maintaining the factory in a productive state have to be charged to each job or contract under the heading of **oncost** or **overhead expense**, generally on a percentage basis over the whole production.

——— Stocks and their turnover ———

Large stocks held in the warehouse do not earn their keep, yet minimum stocks must be maintained, based upon past experience.

The aim of management is to increase the rate of stock turnover, thereby increasing trading profit. Periodic checks are made by the cost accountant (in big industry) comparing the rate of stock turnover with that of earlier periods. An illustration of a small manufacturer's cost statement is now shown, providing useful information for both the cost and financial accounting.

Note how the cost of production fits into the trading account, as shown on the next page, taking the place of the ordinary purchases of a non-manufacturing concern. The comparison of the gross profit ratios between the two periods reflects the general price trend, always rising under inflationary conditions. To maintain existing prices means that many producers and manufacturers are pressurised out of business by their ever-increasing costs.

Cost of Production Statement

	£	£
Stock of raw materials 1 Jan.	8 500	
Purchases of raw material	72 350	
Carriage on raw material	150	
	81 000	
Less stock of raw materials 31 Dec.	10 000	
Raw materials consumed	71 000	
Production wages & NIC	110 000	
Direct expenses of production	2 200	
Prime cost		183 200
Factory overheads:		
Heating and lighting	1 700	
Rent and rates	3 500	
Power	2 400	
Supervision (foremen)	8 800	
Depreciation of machinery	2 000	
Overhead expense		18 400
Cost of production		£201 600

Trading Account for the year ended 31 December

	Current year		Previous year	
	£	£	£	£
Net sales for year		275 000		220 000
Cost of sales				
Stock of finished goods 1 Jan.	32 000		34 000	
Cost of production b/f	201 600		158 800	
	233 600		192 800	
Less stock of finished goods 31 Dec.	36 000		32 000	
	197 600		160 800	
Warehouse wages & NIC	4 400		4 200	
Cost of sales		202 000		165 000
Gross trading profit		£73 000		£55 000

Rate of stock turnover

Current year

$$\frac{202\ 000}{34\ 000} = 5.94 \text{ times in the year}$$

Previous year

$$\frac{165\ 000}{33\ 000} = 5 \text{ times}$$

(approx. every two months)

The gross profit ratios in the above illustration are:

$$\frac{73\ 000}{275\ 000} \times 100 = 26.55\% \text{ for the current year}$$

$$\frac{55\ 000}{220\ 000} \times 100 = 25.00\% \text{ for the previous year.}$$

The increased ratio may be due to a variety of causes – increased prices, reduced level of overheads through greater production, or perhaps more effective control over publicity and administrative expenditure despite the inflationary conditions, etc.

—— Manufacturing accounts ——

The heavy costs and expenses at basic production level determine, to a large degree, the ultimate selling price of the finished product. These bulk costs normally occur long before the retail stage.

The manufacturer must obtain raw materials at world commodity prices, and provide both an efficient labour force and the machinery of production involving heavy capital finance, months ahead of the estimated demand for any marketable product.

The cost of production statement (see page 204) is also a manufacturing account, preceding and leading into the business trading account. Generally, it would comprise a greater list of debit items, all costs and expenses of production, the total being referred to as the **cost of production**. This cost of manufacture or production is brought down to the debit of the trading account we already know, taking the place of the purchases figure to which we have become accustomed. But now that we are about to make up a manufacturing account, remember that some finished goods may have been bought from outside suppliers at this stage. These are shown as an additional debit in the ordinary way.

Several classes of stock

In making up another more detailed manufacturing account, and processing it through to the final net trading profit stage, take note of the three different kinds of stock: raw material, partly finished goods (sometimes called **work in progress**), and finished goods. The latter belongs only to the trading and selling section of the business, whereas the first two type of stocks are found only in the manufacturing or production account. The *closing balances*, however, of all three kinds of stock are eventually taken to join the current assets on the balance sheet.

The old-fashioned style of manufacturing account has been drafted below to emphasise the various 'account' stages and sections and to draw the student's attention to the sectional terms in use – materials consumed, prime cost, factory/works cost, and the cost of sales.

Manufacturing, Trading and Profit and Loss Account for the year ended 31 December

	£			£
Stock of raw materials 1 Jan.	2 000	Work in progress		
Purchases of raw materials	36 000	31 Dec.	£6 000	
Carriage on raw materials	1 000	*less* 1 Jan.	5 500	500
	39 000			
Less stock of raw materials 31 Dec.	5 000	Cost of production c/d		75 840
Materials consumed	34 000			
Direct wages & NIC	30 000			
Direct expenses	6 740			
Prime cost	70 740			
Overhead expense				
including deprec. of plant	5 600			
Factory/works cost	76 340			76 340
Stock of finished goods 1 Jan.	30 000	Net sales		130 000
Cost of production brought down	75 840			
Purchases of finished goods	1 400			
Carriage of finished goods	60			
	107 340			
Less stock of finished goods 31 Dec.	25 000			
Cost of sales	82 340			
Gross profit c/d	47 660			
	130 000			130 000
Carriage outwards	700	Gross profit b/d		47 660
Salaries & NIC	8 800	Discounts received		300
Office expenses	4 400			
Discounts allowed	440			
Advertising	3 120			
Net trading profit	30 500			
	47 960			47 960

Note on the market price of goods manufactured

This type of examination problem is quite straightforward, provided examples have been studied. Sometimes, though, examiners like to add a footnote about the retail value or price of the goods manufactured on the open market.

If, for instance, in addition to all the information above, the examiner had introduced the figure of £90 000 as the approximate market value of the manufactured goods (shown as the cost of production amounting to £75 840), to show an estimated 'profit on manufacture' of £14 160, the simple adjustments to the manufacturing account already illustrated would be as follows.

In place of the cost of production figure of £75 840 on the credit of manufacturing account insert the current market value of £90 000. Carry down and debit this £90 000 to the next section of this account (the trading account) in place of the figure £74 840 for the cost of production.

The estimated profit on manufacture £14 160 will be debited (as the balance of the manufacturing account) and *brought down to the credit of the third section of this combined account*, the profit and loss account.

This is simply a management accounting concept to measure performance and compare production costs with the prices of finished goods on the open market. There is no change in the ultimate and actual net profit.

Assignments

31   Draw up a comparative trading account from the information given below. Ascertain the cost of sales and calculate the rate of stock turnover for both periods.

	Current year £	Previous year £
Raw material consumed	60 000	53 000
Manufacturing wages	77 000	69 000
Warehousing wages	6 000	5 300
Direct expenses	5 000	4 900
Overheads	10 000	8 800
Net sales	240 000	200 000
Stocks of finished goods		
1 January	26 000	25 000
31 December	24 000	26 000

31.2 Prepare a manufacturing account from the following figures, to show clearly:

(a) the raw materials consumed   (b) the prime cost
(c) factory overheads   (d) cost of production.

		Raw material £	Work in progress £
Stocks	1 July (one year ago)	2500	450
	30 June (at year end)	3000	520

	£		£
Manufacturing wages	14 400	Fuel and power	1 500
Indirect wages	4 300	Direct expenses	430
Works manager's		Royalties on production	350
salary	3 000	Deprec. of machinery	200
Raw material		General maintenance	150
purchases	18 700	Insurance of factory	100
Factory rent		Carriage on raw	
and rates	2 200	material	120

31.3 You are required to make up a combined manufacturing, trading and profit and loss account from the following information, and give details of:

(a) materials consumed   (b) cost of production
(c) profit on manufacture   (d) cost of sales
(e) net profit for the year.

		Raw material £	Finished goods £	Work in progress £
Stocks	Jan. 1	1 000	2 375	1 900
	Dec. 31	625	2 760	1 750

	£		£
Salaries	3 350	Carriage outwards	410
Office expenses	1 190	Raw materials purchases	7 500
Factory expenses	3 188	Carriage on material	125
Discounts received	350	Sales less returns	49 000
Advertising	1 800	Warehousing expenses	865
Discounts allowed	300	Purchases/	
Factory wages	12 110	finished goods	1 175

Factory plant and machinery is to be depreciated by £2750. The market value of the actual cost of production at the balance sheet date is estimated at £30 450. This is to be taken into account in drafting the manufacturing account.

32
INTRODUCTION TO LIMITED COMPANIES

Limited liability

The modern form of **limited company** came into common use during the last half of the nineteenth century. The main form of trading vehicle before that had been the sole proprietorship or the partnership, but both of these are unwieldy when the people putting up the capital are different from those actually managing the company. Ostensibly this is the main reason for a limited company – so that someone putting up capital for a venture without the intention of being involved in managing it will only have that limited amount of capital at risk, rather than having unlimited liability against all personal wealth as in the case of a partnership. The limited company is a **legal entity** – a legal 'person' – in its own right, and can be sued for debts owed, breaches of contract etc. But it is a different person from the shareholder or the director, and neither can (in principle) be required to pay money which is owed by the company.

This principle holds true for the large companies quoted on the stock-market, where the shareholders are entirely different from the company and from the directors. However it has to be said that of the million or so 'live' companies currently listed at Companies House, well under 10% will have any real separation between owners and managers. The remaining 90% plus will have shareholders who are also the directors of the company, or are married to the directors. However, they will still be able to maintain the legal position that they are not personally responsible for the debts of the company. The company here is a vehicle for providing limited liability from the creditors of the trade that they themselves carry on through the company, and a means to reduce the tax liability on undistributed profits (companies with profits under £300 000 only pay tax at the equivalent of the personal basic rate of tax on such profits).

However, regardless of the economic reality, the law and accounting procedures governing a limited company rely on the principle that ownership and management are two entirely different functions.

Owners and managers

The owners of a limited liability company are the **shareholders**. They each own a number of shares in the company, and their entitlement to share in the profits of the company depends on the proportion of the total issued shares that they own.

The shares will normally carry voting rights, again in proportion to the number of shares owned. So if a company has issued 100 ordinary shares, 80 of them held by one person and 20 other people each holding one share, the shareholder with 80 shares can outvote all the other 20 put together.

The shareholders, meeting in an annual meeting, will elect directors to manage the company on their behalf. These are the managers of the company, although some may only have a part-time role centred on attending board meetings (known as **non-executive directors**).

It should be apparent that the role of the financial statements in this respect is crucial, since they are the main way in which the shareholders, who are not involved in the day-to-day operation of the company, can see how the managers are carrying out their job. Because of this, there are detailed statutory rules on how the accounts of a limited company should be set out. These are contained in the Companies Act 1985 as amended by the Companies Act 1989.

Additionally, limited companies may have to have an annual **audit**, where their financial statements are checked by an independent firm of accountants, who give an opinion as to whether they give a true and fair view. Smaller companies need not have an audit if the shareholders agree to do without one; normally it is companies where the shareholders are also directors who take advantage of this.

—— Capital of a limited company ——

The constitution and rules of a company are contained in two documents called the **Memorandum** and **Articles**. These set out the types of share capital the company is entitled to issue, and the rules governing the voting of shareholders and the relationship of shareholders to the company.

In the simplest type of capital structure, a company has the right to issue a given number of ordinary shares (its **authorised share capital**) which it has actually issued (its **issued share capital**) to shareholders, who have paid in full the price put on the share by the company. For example, a company might have an authorised share capital of one hundred £1 shares which it has issued equally to two shareholders, A and B, who have each paid £50 for their fifty shares. The company has an authorised, issued and fully paid share capital of £100. If the company were now to be unable to pay its debts, the shares would become worthless, but A and B would not have to pay out anything further.

The most common variation from this is that the issued share capital is less than the authorised share capital. So in the above example, A and B might only have taken one share each, paying £1 each, with no other shares being issued. They would still each own half of the company, and are each entitled to half of the profits from it, but the company would only have £2 in its bank account instead of the £100 it raised previously. The shares are still fully paid, and if the company could not pay its debts neither A nor B would be obliged to pay any more of their money in. The only difference that having the unissued shares makes is that the company does not have to alter its memorandum if it wants to issue more shares.

Partly paid capital is another matter. Instead of the last example, A and B might have each taken the fifty shares, but only paid 2p in the pound for each of them. This is called **partly paid capital**. 2p each for fifty shares means that they would have paid £1 in total just as in the last example, and they would each own half of the company and be entitled to half of the profits. But this time, if the company were unable to pay its debts, A and B would be liable to pay the outstanding capital of 98p a share, giving them each a liability of £49. This would, however, be the limit of their liability. It is comparatively rare to have partly paid share capital except where the price of shares is paid in instalments in a public issue.

Shares give the shareholder a right to receive a share of the profits, but only when it is agreed to make a distribution of them. This distribution is called a **dividend** and will be declared as so much per share. The decision on payment of a dividend is taken at the Annual General Meeting, although in practice for a stock market company it is the directors who decide how much is to be paid out. Shares can normally be bought and sold freely, but they are only worth whatever someone is prepared to pay for them. Unless they are specifically issued as redeemable shares (which is not normal) they need never be repaid by the company.

Loan capital

Companies may also raise money by borrowing it. Sometimes they will simply borrow from a bank, but sometimes they will issue loan certificates, known as **debentures**, sometimes called **loan stock**. These normally carry a fixed rate of interest, and a right to have the capital repaid at a certain time.

For example, a company might issue £10 000 8% debentures redeemable in 2010. That means that it will receive £10 000 from the people who originally buy the debentures, but every year until 2010 it must pay the holders interest totalling £800. In 2010 the £10 000 must be repaid to the debenture holders. This is regardless of whether or not profits are made by the company; on the other hand, the debenture holders have no right to any further income regardless of how well the company performs.

The accounting entries for the issue of various types of capital are considered in the next chapter, but in the meantime it is important to understand the differences between the financial statements of a limited company and a sole trader.

Characteristics of limited company accounts

There are two main areas of difference – what happens after net profit in the profit and loss account, and what is shown in capital on the balance sheet.

Having calculated net profit as for sole proprietors, this is taken down to an appropriation account, which shows how the profit is to be appropriated.

The first thing to be taken off is *corporation tax due*, to give *profit after tax*. Next any *balance brought forward* from previous years is added. The *dividends proposed on the shares* are then deducted, and finally a *balance of profit brought forward* is left. It is illegal for a company to distribute more than it has in total profit, both earned in the year and brought forward.

Example

Limited company appropriation account	
Net profit	10 000
less corporation tax	2 400
	7 600
add retained profit b/f	4 000
	11 600
less dividend proposed	8 000
Retained profit c/f	3 600

On the balance sheet, the share capital appears separately from the brought forward profits, but all of them are still shareholders' funds. The brought forward profits are sometimes called **reserves**, although there are also other credit balances that can be referred to in this way.

33
ACCOUNTING FOR SHARE CAPITAL

Registered and issued share capital

The nominal, authorised or registered share capital is that stated in the company's charter, the Memorandum of Association. That part of the authorised capital which is issued to the public is shown under the heading of issued capital on the balance sheet in this manner.

Authorised and issued share capital	£	£
Authorised capital		
100 000 10% preference shares of £1 each	100 000	
400 000 ordinary shares of 50p each	<u>200 000</u>	<u>300 000</u>
Issued capital		
100 000 10% preference shares of £1 each fully paid	100 000	
300 000 ordinary shares of 50p each fully paid	<u>150 000</u>	250 000

Note that it is only the issued share capital which forms part of the double entry system, and consequently the authorised capital is ruled off when it has not been fully issued.

There are various categories of capital. In the figures shown above, the nominal, registered or authorised capital is £300 000. The issued capital is £250 000, consisting of 100 000 10% preference shares fully called and paid up, and 300 000 ordinary shares of 50p called and paid up. The uncalled capital of 100 000 ordinary shares of 50p has not yet been issued to the public.

There are also various classes of shares, the two main classes being preference and ordinary. The former carries a fixed rate of interest which is payable, dependent upon the company's available profits, *before* the payment of any dividend recommended by the directors to ordinary shareholders.

Share certificates are issued to the company members. The name of each shareholder is also entered on the members' register to show the registered numbers of his or her holding. From time to time, when shares are bought and sold through the medium of the stock exchange, the name of the 'old' member is erased from company records and a new certificate issued under the seal of the company showing the holding of the 'new' member.

Share issues

With most public share issues, it is customary for the payment of the shares taken up to be made by instalments, in the following manner.

A new company is 'floated' with an authorised share capital of 200 000 ordinary shares of £1 each. Half of the registered capital is to be offered to the general public and to be paid in three distinct stages, thus:

20p on application by 30 April
30p on allotment on 1 June
50p first and final call on 1 July.

The build-up of the company's finances is now shown over these two months. No complications are assumed (refunds, unpaid calls, etc.). The money comes in direct to the company's bank account, and the ordinary share capital is built up this way, via application, allotment and final call accounts:

CASH BOOK Bank receipts (debit) side

		30 April	1 June	1 July	Total
		£	£	£	£
Application a/c		20 000			20 000
Allotment a/c			30 000		50 000
Call a/c				50 000	100 000

Ordinary Share Capital (credit) side

	30 April	1 June	1 July	Total
	£	£	£	£
Application a/c	20 000			20 000
Allotment a/c		30 000		50 000
Call a/c			50 000	100 000

Assuming that no trading operations have yet taken place, the company balance sheet on 1 July appears as follows.

Assets of the company
Bank account   £100 000

Represented by
Authorised share capital
200 000 ordinary shares of £1 each   £200 000

Issued share capital
100 000 ordinary shares of £1 fully paid   £100 000

—— Application and allotment ——

This is a general guide to the double entry procedure.

		Debit	Credit
(a)	Completed forms for the purchase of shares and application money received from the general public.	Bank	Application account
(b)	Company confirms allotment to successful applicants –	Applic. a/c	Share capital a/c
(c)	and asks for amounts due on allotments.	Allot. a/c	Share capital
(d)	Some money may be returned to unsuccessful applicants with letters of regret.	Applic. a/c	Bank
(e)	Allotment money comes in.	Bank	Allotment account
(f)	If some money is unpaid (owing) on allotment.	Calls in arrear	Allotment a/c
(g)	The directors decide to make a call for further money.	Call account	Share capital
(h)	The call money comes in.	Bank	Call account
(I)	If some calls are unpaid (owing).	Calls in arrear	Call account

Application and allotment accounts are generally combined.

Note that after the application stage, the share capital of the company is *credited before the money is actually received* on the allotment and call accounts.

Calls in arrear

The liability of a company member is limited to the amount he (or she) has contracted to pay for the shareholding. If he has not paid all the 'calls' made on him by the company, he becomes a debtor for the money that is due. Sums owing by a defaulting shareholder are referred to as **calls in arrear**.

If, in the last illustration, John Brown failed to pay the final call of 50p on his allotted 500 shares, he would become a debtor of the company for £250 (50p on 500 £1 shares).

The share capital at 1 July would show the full credit balance of £100 000, but cash would be short by £250.

In making up the company's balance sheet at 1 July, John Brown's debt would not be included in the ordinary trade debtors' total in the current assets, but would be deducted as 'calls in arrear' from the issued share capital in this manner:

Assets of the company			
Bank account			£99 750
Represented by			
Authorised share capital			
200 000 ordinary shares of £1 each		£200 000	
Issued share capital			
100 000 ordinary shares of £1 fully paid		£100 000	
	Less calls in arrear	250	£99 750

The directors of the company will give John Brown notice that unless he pays his final call of £250 by a certain date, his shares will be forfeited and sold (probably to another member). No refund would be made of the amount he has already paid.

Premium on shares

A successful company, probably needing further capital for expansion, might put out an additional issue of shares at a **premium**, i.e. at an amount above the nominal or par value of the shares. If, for instance, the nominal value of the shares was £1 and they were issued at £1.20 per share, the premium would be 20%. An applicant for 100 shares would pay £120 for them.

The Companies Acts require amounts received as premiums on shares to be taken to a share premium account as a capital reserve. This kind of reserve can only be used for special purposes (such as off-setting capital losses) and is not available for transfer to the credit of the revenue account and to be used for payment as a dividend, as in the case of a general reserve.

Normally the premium is paid with the allotment money, the book entries, in the first instance, being the full debit to the allotment account, with the separate amounts being credited to share capital and the share premium account. Then, when the allotment money (and the premium) is received, the bank is debited and the allotment account credited with the full amount of the allotment money plus the premium.

The premium, as a credit balance in the books, is shown on the balance sheet under the separate heading of *capital reserve*, between the issued capital and the revenue reserves, thus:

Authorised and issued share capital		
200 000 ordinary shares of £1 fully paid		£200 000
Capital reserve		
Share premium account		10 000
Revenue reserves		
General reserve account	£25 000	
Profit and loss undistributed balance	8 000	33 000

Debentures

A debenture issue is similar to a share issue, often by instalments, and it is referred to as **loan capital**. Generally, on the vertical style balance sheet, the total figure for debentures is deducted from the total of the *net assets* to give the net worth or equity of the company (see the end of the next chapter).

Assignments

33.1 The Colby Mail Order Company Limited was registered on 1 January with an authorised share capital of £200 000 in ordinary shares of £1. On 1 February, one-hundred thousand shares were offered for public subscription by instalments as follows:

On application	10p per share
On allotment	20p per share
On 25 March	30p on first call
On 20 June	40p second and final call

The issue was fully subscribed. All monies were received on the due dates with the exception of the second and final call of one member, a Mr Frank Evans, who had been allotted 1000 shares.

Journalise the accounting entries and make up the balance sheet of the company, in so far as these particulars are concerned, as at 20 June.

33.2 Jaybee Enterprises Ltd issued 200 000 Ordinary Shares of £1 at a premium of 10%, and also £60 000 12% debentures at par.

Applications were received for 212 000 shares. The money surplus to the company's requirements was sent back with 'letters of regret' to those applicants who had asked only for small batches of shares.

The shares were received in three instalments: 20p on application, 40p on allotment (including the premium), and 50p two months after allotment. All monies were received on the share issue except in the case of one shareholder of 400 shares who could not meet his final call. The Board decided to allow this member another month to pay the amount outstanding, otherwise his shares were to be forfeited.

The debenture issue was subscribed in full and all monies banked.

Write up the cash book of the company and all relevant ledger accounts, and show the balance sheet, incorporating these details, made up on 30 September, the day after the date set for the final call.

33.3 Is there any difference between these three terms:

(*a*) registered capital, (*b*) authorised capital, (*c*) nominal capital?

34

THE FINAL
ACCOUNTS OF A
LIMITED COMPANY

This chapter, on company accounts, is still introductory and simply intended to cover the requirements of the first-level Accounting examination syllabuses.

The 'published section' of the profit and loss account

The Companies Act 1985 provides a rigid hierarchy of headings which must be used in reporting the results of a limited company. The main headings for a profit and loss account, for example, begin as follows:

- Turnover
- Cost of Sales
- Gross profit or loss
- Distribution costs
- Administrative expenses.

The Companies Acts also require full public disclosure of certain items which are normally included as notes. Full details must be given of directors' fees and salaries, loan and debenture interest, and the depreciation of fixed assets.

Information must also be given of the following 'appropriations' of profit:

- amounts paid or reserved for taxation
- dividends paid or recommended
- amounts transferred to (or withdrawn from) reserves.

The purpose of these disclosures is for the benefit of the shareholders, creditors, debenture holders and the Inland Revenue.

—— Balance sheet disclosures ——

The format for the balance sheet is equally rigid, for example, with Fixed Assets normally forming the opening item, split into intangible, tangible and investments, and each of these further divided into four or more categories.

The detailed requirements of the Companies Acts need not be memorised at this level of study. The next few paragraphs are included by way of interest, emphasising the fair and common sense aspects of much of the recent legislation to ensure that the final accounts of the limited companies, financed to a large extent with the savings of many thousands of ordinary people, do, in fact, 'show a true and fair view' of the finances of each limited company.

The authorised share capital, where it is a different amount to the issued share capital, is simply presented for information and ruled off as it does not form part of the double entry.

Capital and revenue reserves are to be shown under separate headings. The former cannot be paid away in dividend, whereas the latter can be written back to the credit of profit and loss appropriation account if recommended by directors and approved by members.

Long-term liabilities are to be shown under their own headings. Current liabilities will include any bank overdraft, loan and debenture interest owing, expense accruals, and *dividends proposed but not yet paid*.

Notes detail any arrears of dividend of certain types of shares (cumulative preference shares); also details of any contingent liabilities, and capital expenditure authorised by the directors.

A company's fixed assets are shown at *cost less aggregate depreciation written off*. The fixed assets are grouped in order of permanency (land, buildings, plant and machinery, fittings and fixtures, motor vehicles) and totalled separately from the current assets.

Current assets are generally shown in this order: stock on hand at the date of the balance sheet, trade debtors, pre-payments such as rates in advance, and the bank and cash balances.

Notes are to be made of acquisitions or disposals of fixed assets during the year, and a statement made of the method of arriving at the valuation of the stock of finished goods and the work in progress.

The vertical presentation of the balance sheet discloses the working capital, net assets and the equity of the company at a glance.

The auditor's report is usually attached to the balance sheet, generally confirming that it depicts a 'true and fair view' of the company's financial affairs and complies with the requirements of the Companies Acts. A qualified report is issued when the auditors are not satisfied about some issues, and is generally a warning for shareholders to ask questions.

Auditors do not prepare the final accounts of the company and are not employed by the company. They belong to a completely separate and distinct firm of professional accountants.

A full example of published company accounts has not been included here, as it would have to be over-simplified to reproduce it. Instead, students are urged to look at the financial statements of quoted companies to see how they are laid out. Large public libraries hold these and the *Financial Times* carries details on its share price page of a free service for obtaining copies of accounts.

Assignments

34.1 Make up the profit and loss account, including a separate 'published section', of the Kaypec Trading Co. Ltd from the following information:

	£
Turnover (net sales) for the year ended 31 December	380 000
Gross trading profit for the year	168 900
Undistributed profit from previous year	4 500
Rent and rates	8 600
Bad debts written off	460
Insurance paid	380
Commissions received	7 400
Directors' fees	10 000
Salaries of directors	16 000
Office salaries and NIC	37 500
Depreciation of vehicles	3 250
Half year's preference dividend paid June 30	5 000
Advertising and publicity	3 520
Audit fee payable	2 000

Adjustments are to be made for the following:

> Payments in advance: rates £1400; insurance £80
> Commissions earned, not yet received £720
> Provision for Corporation Tax £40 000
> Increase of bad debts provision by £150 to £1000.

The directors recommend the payment of the second half of the preference dividend, and the transfer of £8000 to general reserve. They further recommend a dividend of 15% to ordinary shareholders amounting to £30 000, and ask for the approval of members for the writing off of one-third of the formation expenses debit, standing in the books at £4800.

34.2 The MM Company Limited was registered with an authorised capital of £50 000 in 100 000 ordinary shares of 50p each. All the capital had been issued and was fully paid.

You are required to draw up the balance sheet of the company from the information below.

	£
Plant and machinery (cost £30 000; depreciation to date £12 500)	17 500
Van (cost £3400; depreciation to date £1850)	1 550
Freehold premises at cost	34 000
Credit balance on profit and loss of undistributed profit	5 660
General reserve account	4 000
Trade debtors and creditors £6400:£4230	
Wages owing £440 Rates in advance £320	
Stock on hand at 30 June	16 500
Bank overdraft at 30 June	300
Provision for bad debts	640
Provision for Corporation Tax	10 000
Investments held by the Company (9% Treasury Stock, present market value £2800)	3 000
Ordinary dividend recommended by directors at 8%	4 000

35
ACCOUNTING
STANDARDS

Most of this book sets out one way, and one way only, of entering a particular transaction. However, if you move to higher level examinations you will find that for many accounting transactions there are potentially several different ways in which they could be recorded.

For example, in all the examples given so far, you have been provided with a figure for depreciation. But how should the rate of depreciation be set? Is it acceptable to change from one method of depreciation to another? Should buildings be depreciated, on the grounds that they eventually become uneconomic to repair or adapt and have to be torn down and rebuilt, when in practice the rise in value of the land they stand on has tended to outstrip the loss in value of the building itself?

It is important that there is consistency between organisations, especially quoted companies, in the way that such transactions are recorded. If there is not, there is no realistic way that the financial statements can be used to compare one with another unless a great deal of background information is given and analysed.

Accounting standards

While legislation may provide some uniformity, the accountancy profession has also responded by setting up the **Accounting Standards Board** (ASB) which issues binding guidance on how certain transactions should be accounted for and reported. From the 1970s onwards the ASB produced 25 **Statements of Standard Accounting Practice** (SSAPs) on subjects as diverse as disclosure of accounting policies, accounting for depreciation, and accounting for goodwill.

In 1990 the composition of the ASB was changed, making it more independent of the accountancy institutes which set it up. It is now issuing **Financial Reporting Standards** (FRSs), and the intention is that these will eventually replace all the existing SSAPs. Until then, the SSAPs remain in force.

There is a noticeable tendency in the FRSs to issue statements of principle rather than specific accountancy treatments. This seems to have come about because companies and their auditors were attending more to the letter of the SSAPs and not to the principle that they were trying to enforce. Thus for example FRS 5 lays down the general principle that *the substance and not the form of a transaction should be reported in the balance sheet*, and then gives guidance on how that should be implemented, whereas SSAP 24 (although it still remains in force) represents an earlier attempt to get certain equipment lease contracts reclassified as purchases. Whereas SSAP 24 could be avoided by rewriting the terms of the lease, it is less easy to avoid the general principles involved in FRS 5.

International Standards

Whilst it is important to compare accounts of companies within the same country, it is also important to compare them on an international basis, and the importance of this increases as the internationalisation of economics increases. In 1973 the **International Accounting Standards Committee** was formed to harmonise standard-setting internationally. Whilst the standards it produces do not have binding force, it is normal for their provisions to be followed in the Financial Reporting Standards issued by the ASB. Any deviation will be specifically stated in the standard.

Inflation accounting

One particular problem for the standard-setters has been inflation accounting. The effects of inflation, particularly high inflation, on historical cost accounts can be substantial. Stock purchased some years earlier which is eventually sold may seem to have generated a high profit because inflation has increased the price. However, the cost of replacing the stock would now also be very high. The historical accounting system would seem here to reward holding onto slow-moving stock, which is not generally a laudable objective.

The cost of assets wearing out is reflected in historical accounting through depreciation, which charges a proportion of their cost to the profit and loss account each year. However, the cost of replacing the asset with a new one will be far higher if inflation has increased prices substantially.

There was an SSAP that required the use of a new approach to this problem, called **current value accounting**. SSAP 14 was formulated in the late 1970s, when inflation had been very high. Unfortunately it was considered excessively complex and the financial statements that resulted from applying it were felt to be uninformative. This dislike may have been partly to do with the fact that profits reported under current value accounting were invariably lower than those under historical cost accounting during a period of inflation.

The standard was simply not applied by most companies, and although auditors duly commented in their audit opinions that the standard had not been complied with, there was nothing that could be done to enforce compliance. Eventually in the mid-1980s inflation came down substantially and the standard was eventually dropped.

There are two lessons from the story of SSAP 14. The first is that, despite the undoubted problems caused by inflation when looking at historical cost accounting, it is extremely difficult to get agreement on making changes. The second is that if an accounting standard encounters widespread resistance it will simply cease to be effective – it is effective only because it is generally agreed.

Smaller companies

An increasingly relevant issue as accounting standards proliferate is the applicability of them to smaller companies. Small companies and their accountants complain that the standard setting process is geared to rooting out sophisticated massaging of the figures by large quoted companies, yet the standards are applied with equal rigour to small companies that simply do not need them.

The ASB has approached this by drafting a single standard for smaller companies that includes the key elements of the other standards but excludes some of the more obscure and irrelevant sections. It remains to be seen how effective this will be.

36
NON-FINANCIAL REPORTING

It is appropriate to conclude the book by pointing out the limitations of traditional accounting. The opening page pointed out that accounting was the *arithmetic of commerce* and as a result accountancy finds it hard to deal with anything that cannot be reduced to financial figures.

Nevertheless, it is clear that there are other concerns which someone reviewing the activities of a company or other organisation might have. Many investors are now concerned to ensure that they only invest in companies that do not pollute the environment. Trades unions in particular will want to ensure that any investments made by their pension or hardship funds only go to companies with good labour relations. There is a wide and growing range of factors which many experts feel should be capable of reflection in the accounting process. These concepts are given the general term **social accounting**, although there is little agreement on how broad the spectrum covered by the term really is.

It has to be admitted that at present this is a concern primarily at the academic and research level rather than one which is being put into practice. Most businesses consider that labour relations are still the remit of the Human Resources Department not the Finance Department. Companies are far more likely to undertake a review of energy efficiency because they want to save money than because they want to save the planet from global warming. However, there is a growing belief that in the foreseeable future some mechanism will have to be found that imposes a genuine requirement on businesses to account for their actions in more than financial terms. In any case, the non-financial aspects of a business can have important financial consequences long-term that are not recognised in the normal process of accounting.

Two of the main areas where social accounting is relevant are labour relations and the environment. These are considered below

Labour relations

Businesses will frequently say 'we *are* our people' – the business is only as good as the people it employs. In some businesses this is quite literally true: a company writing software for computer games may be totally dependent on the skills of its programmers. If they were all to leave, the company would be left with nothing but a few second-hand computers, and possibly some royalties from previous programs.

It may be thought strange, then, that traditional accounting actually discriminates against good employers in the short term. Consider two companies writing games software – Setendo Ltd and Ninga Ltd, each employing ten programmers on the same market rate of pay. In the first year they each produce a program, and the programs sell equally well. However, Setendo lays off half of its work force as the project nears completion after nine months, because it only needs five of them to finish it off. Ninga retains all its staff, even though there is not enough work for them in the last three months. At the beginning of the next year each company starts to write another program, and Setendo rehires five more programmers to bring the total back up to ten. This pattern is repeated for several years. What is the accounting outcome?

Initially Setendo Ltd will probably report better results than Ninga Ltd – its wage bill will be lower because it lays off staff when they are not working at full stretch. However, in the long run it may find it more and more difficult to hire good staff. Word will get round in the industry that you are far better off working or Ninga, because you don't have the threat of redundancy hanging over your head every year. Gradually the best programmers will end up at Ninga and the second best at Setendo, Ninga will start producing better games than Setendo, and will sell more copies and make more profits.

Of course this idealised scenario does not always work out neatly. There may be such a shortage of jobs and so many good programmers that Setendo will always be able to recruit good staff, and will always make higher profits on a traditional accounting basis. However this does not mean that there are no adverse consequences. The stress caused by the continual layoffs may mean that some of the programmers become ill, requiring medical help from the state. Being unemployed for three months a year means that programmers will be claiming social security benefits. It may cause problems in their family lives, leading to marital breakups. In general it can be said that Ninga Ltd's policies have a greater social benefit to the community at large than Setendo's do. This cannot be recognised properly in financial statements.

Occasionally there are attempts to introduce some form of labour relations recognition into financial reporting, for example by requiring businesses to state the percentage of their workforce which is disabled. Partly this is ineffective because companies come up with stock phrases and words that limit the effectiveness of such disclosures, but mainly it is ineffective because the overwhelming majority of investors and other users of the accounts pay no attention to it.

Ecological reporting

There is perhaps a greater interest in ecological measures because it can have an impact on investment. Although the number of investors and investment funds which will not invest in ecologically unsound companies is still small, it is growing, and there are now research bodies who analyse the results of companies to produce information for ecologically-aware investors to act on. They also produce information about other ethical issues such as involvement in the arms, tobacco or alcohol trades, any or all of which may be important to ethical investors. The perception of a company as ecologically friendly may also help sell its products, as consumers are more aware of the ecological impact of their purchases.

Again the implication may be both long-term financial to the company or a cost to the community at large. A company which uses a non-renewable source of wood for its products may make higher profits in the short term because it is the cheapest source of supply. In the long term it may find that as the supply dries up the price goes up, but even if the supply is so substantial that it outlasts the company's need for it, the environment as a whole will have suffered from the loss of the trees. The former will eventually be recognised in the accounts, but will not impact in the early years; the latter would not be recognised at all.

The main way in which ecological concerns are being brought into financial accounting is by putting a financial cost on them. By raising the taxes on car and lorry fuel, governments can encourage businesses to limit the amount of pollution they cause by travel. Providing subsidies for rail freight can switch goods from road to rail, even if road would otherwise be cheaper for the company. Imposing a tax on land fill encourages companies to recycle more of their waste, and to put pressure on their suppliers to reduce packaging etc.

– Other aspects of social accounting –

Ecological concerns and **labour relations** are two of the biggest elements of social accounting, but they are not the only ones. Good relations with a local community is another area often commented on – does the company involve itself with local schools and voluntary organisations? Is it aware of its responsibility to the local community not to close down a factory and create high employment? Again this can have a financial effect on the company long-term in the retention of labour and goodwill among local customers, and it can *also* have a financial impact on the community as a whole.

There is also a wider aspect to social accounting on a national or international level. Growth in the economy is generally reckoned to be a 'good thing', and is certainly recorded as such in the national accounts; it produces a higher rate of **Gross National Product**, or GNP. However it can be argued that continued growth cannot be sustained without excessive damage to the environment and to health by pollution, and that we have insufficiently sophisticated systems for measuring this.

Coventry University

ANSWERS

Answers to Assignments and Revision Exercises

2.1 £45.56   **3.2** £117.15   **3.3** £316.14   **4.1** £92.30

4.2 £99.97   **5.1** £720   **5.2** CB £48.20; TB £501.50

Revision Exercise 1   CB £269.50; TB £725.84

6.1 COS £4300; GP £3000   **6.2** GP £2130

7.1 GP £1570; NP £1180   **7.2** GP £2570; NP £1920

8.1 Profit £4850   **8.2** TB £6650; GP £1073; NP £510

9 CB £104; TB £2463; GP £477; NP £314; Cap. £1714; BS £1714

10.1 C £35.42; £477.10   **10.2** £10; £516.50

11.2 Debit balance £22.84   **12.1** PC bal. £13.57; refund £16.43

12.2 PC £7.41; refund £27.59   **13.1** PDB £203.50; creditors £111

13.2 PDB £141.60; cash £123.40, bank £559.05; TB £1462.40

14.2 PDB £86; SDB £93.30; cash £20; bank £558.10; TB £1132.20

15.1 Debit £72.20

17.2 £95 credit   **17.3** £40.90 debit

Revision Exercise 2.1   Cash £30; bank £1990.10; TB £3891.40

18.1 GP £264.40; NP £196.40; cap. £3106.40; BS £3310.40

18.2 TB £11 024; GP £4939; NP £2587; cap. £3787; WC £2607;
   BS £4007

19.1 GP on sales 40%; NP on sales 30%; stockturn 5 times in month

Revision Exercise 3   Cash £25; bank £457; TB £10 290; GP £57;
   net loss £74; cap. £5826; BS £8956

21.1 GP £3294; NP £1828

22.1 Capital £7500

Revision Exercise 4   TB £10 434; cash £20; bank £421; GP £229;
   NP £168; cap. £5768; BS £9902

23.1 £180

23.2 Lease £6400; deprec. £000 p n ; Machinery £2890; deprec. £600 and £510

23.3 NP £3814; deprec. £1166; cap. £7314; BS £10 004

24.1 Prov. increase £75; bad debts £8

24.2 Prov. decrease £70; bad debts £54

24.3 Prov. decrease £14; bad debts £30

25.1 In advance £66; revenue £72

25.2 revenue £19 106; creditors for wages £662

25.3 Revenue £218; creditors £38; Revenue £195; in advance £65

Examination Exercise   **2** Claim £3510   **3** GP £7442; NP £2903; cap. £9923; BS £11 308   **5** Asset balance £612   **6** 20 Main Street

26.1 NP £3792; BS £2995   **26.2** NP £240; BS £7180

26.3 NP £14 070; BS £24 210   **27.1** CB £172.10

27.2 Surplus £411; BS £4435   **28.1** Dr. £40; cr. £44 205

28.2 BL £3267; SL £3939   **29.1** M £790; L £560

29.2 A £1100; B £500; C £100   **29.3** SP £8700; MD £3700; BS £14 150

Revision Exercise 5   **1** CB £744; subs £931; deficit £197; BS £1450   **2** GP £8995; NP £5065; BS £13 215; current accounts JM £390, PR £50; WC £3630

31.1 C of P £152 000:£135 700; COS £160 000:£140 000; GP % 33⅓:30; stockturn 6.4:5.5   **31.2** £18 320; £33 500; £11 450; £44 880

31.3 £8000; £26 198; £4252; £32 105; £14 447

33.1 P&L £127 890; published section c/f £11 540

33.2 WC £3610; net assets £59 660

INDEX